The Medicine of Prayer

The Medicine

of Prayer

A Journey of Faith to
Live a Life of Purpose

Litefoot

Published by Litefoot Enterprises, LLC, Seattle, Washington

Edited by Valerie Woods

Front and back cover background photo credit: Dolly Norton

Front cover Litefoot photo credit: Shay Peretz for Litefoot Enterprises, LLC

ISBN: 978-0-9831524-0-8

Printed in the United States of America

First Edition

I pray that those who read this book will be empowered, strengthened & motivated!

I dedicate this book to my beautiful wife Carmen and my two incredible sons Quannah and Sequoyah.

Acknowledgments

Foundation

I would like to thank my parents, Gary and Olga Davis, for instilling within me a great sense of purpose and providing me with inspiration by your actions. For teaching me to set my goals beyond what others think is possible. Thank you for doing all that you could do with the means that you had at your disposal. Most of all thank you for encouraging me to be ME and laying the foundation in my life for what would become The Medicine of Prayer. I am because of you both.

To my grandparents, Roy and Helen Davis, for providing me with such a rich childhood of memories and offering me your insights. Thank you for believing in me and expecting a higher standard from me. Thank you for all the talks and for being patient with me. I carry you both with me still and I know you are never far away. Thank you for watching over me and I hope I have made you proud.

I would like to thank my sister, Angelique Elan Davis, for your enduring love and support. I know that all too often it seems that my life has superseded your dreams and goals. Growing up, I would have thought that you would have been the one on stage first. You are the singer, the songwriter, the performer and the actress. It is you who had these talents first and who unselfishly encouraged me to always be better than I thought I could be. It is you who always helped out everyone else and made sure the home front was okay. Who would have ever known this is the way that it all would turn out? But the Creator makes no mistakes. Please know that you are appreciated beyond words and that I love you with all my heart. We have been through so much and I don't forget. It was you who handed me the microphone from your stand and I thank you for being there for me and encouraging me toward my destiny.

Cultivation

I would like to thank my teachers, coaches, mentors, colleagues, extended family and friends who have helped mold and shape me. There are truly so many of you who have spent hours teaching, inspiring, motivating and encouraging me. There are simply not enough words for me to express my gratitude and humility for all that you have done. I appreciate you all and I am honored to enjoy your continued support. Thank you all for caring!

I would like to thank my ancestors, all tribal nations and the multitudes of tribal citizens who comprise *Indian Country*. Thank you for believing in me. You have been my motivation and you remain my passion. My people are my life. I thank the Creator every day that I have been blessed to be able to serve you. Without you there would be no me and I look forward to continuing to give my all for the future generations of our people and all people.

To my editor and friend, Ms. Valerie Woods, for being such a wonderful and beautiful person. For knowing me and my purpose so well that you were able to help me capture the voice that best tells my story. You have been an inspiration and gift to me and my family. We are grateful for you and the blessing of having you in our lives! You are without a doubt a blessing to us from the Creator. Thank you a thousand times over.

Inspiration

I would like to thank my beautiful wife Carmen and my two wonderful children, Quannah and Sequoyah. I recognize you each as my special gifts from the Creator. I cherish you and honor you with my life.

To the maker of all things, our Grandfather – The Creator -- Thank you for giving me a purpose and for making my life meaningful. For it begins and ends with You. I am nothing without Your guidance and wisdom. I remain committed to running and never walking. To giving You my all. You continue to reveal Your plan for me. You have given me a future and a hope and it has been for good and not for evil. I am yours to mold, shape and use. I am Your child. Please continue to teach and raise me in Your way.

Contents

Foreword

By
J.L. Hughes
On Behalf of the Stoney Nakoda Nation
Morley, Alberta, Canada

"We survive through Prayer. Our religion was given to us by the Creator. We pray to one God and respect all people. This, is our strength." – Chiniki Elder Clifford Powderface.

This book is for all First Nations people, for those who seek the guidance of the Creator, and for all inhabitants of Mother Earth. It contains the distilled wisdom of a thousand years, many elders, and one great man on a mission to reinvigorate his people through the supreme source of power, prayer. To read it is to reclaim the medicine of life, to embark on a journey to Self-Sustainability, and access the simplistic blueprint for fortifying our world and ourselves.

"This message cannot be said enough, communicated enough, or spread enough," says Litefoot. "We have to show those without faith *The Medicine of Prayer* by living it, not just talking about it. That's the reason for this book."

Although the architects for this teaching are many, the hands of the Creator crafted the masterpiece and it is the discovery of lost treasure in Indian country. It is the purest wisdom imparted for those ready to live life larger. The return to traditional spiritual teaching gained momentum following Chief John Snow's creation of the Ecumenical Conference in 1971 – a gathering based in the reestablishing of spirituality as priority in Indian country and among all people.

"This book is in keeping with the energy and thoughts that created that movement," says Litefoot. "It speaks to the value of it, not just for people in Morley, Alberta and other communities, but throughout Indian country and around the world."

Previous to its rebirth, traditional spiritual practices and ceremonies had been outlawed. Their revival commenced when the laws changed throughout North America. Rights once denied were returned and prejudicial laws were repealed. "We were able to exercise our right to pray, our right to spirituality, the rights we should have had all along," says John Snow Jr., who attended his father's first Ecumenical Conference and those thereafter. "Our prayers and ceremonies were returned to our people and everyone came to participate. The elders, from everywhere, said 'take this back to your people and learn to pray in your homeland.' It spread throughout North America from there."

Many directly associate the loss of spirituality with worsening conditions within their communities and in society as a whole. Shortfalls from housing to healthcare and oversights in fundamental components for future growth and stability, such as education and financial security, can be attributed to many things but none more relevant than the absence of a spiritually guided approach.

"When we discuss strife and conflict in the world right now–in the United States and Canada–you can see those are areas where prayer is not a mainstay," says Litefoot. "The power of the Creator or spirituality isn't being held in the esteem that it should be.

"There's nothing on this Earth greater than the Creator, so for us to exclude Him from the equation will only be met with failed results."

The state of humanity and the planet reflects this truth in a mirror of suffering. The *Medicine of Prayer* presents the right action to attune with healing and peace.

Simply stated, the essence of this teaching is a return to age-old cultural practices that grant tremendous power and bestow personal responsibility for the future success of our lives, community, and world. It is the duty of today's leaders to bring this message home.

"It's unfortunate to know that sometimes it takes desperate measures to come back to that which has always been right in front of us," Litefoot added. "Spirituality is the commonality. It's what distinguishes us as a people. It's also the common denominator for all people."

Surviving independently on their lands for centuries by caring for the environment, animals, and each other with a naturally born respect and humility once seemed straightforward. In times of hardship First Nations people relied on the Creator for guidance and strength.

"Modern society has posed a distraction and we have to focus more on traditional ways so new generations don't suffer the consequences of a failed system," says Chief David Bearspaw of Bearspaw First Nation.

To lead today's youth on a precise path that solidifies their independence and offers new found potential, chiefs and elders must openly partake in spiritual practices and bestow their wisdom wherever and whenever possible.

"Being open about having prayer be an integral part of the governing is an incredible benefit to the community. It's not being done nearly enough and I think the return to that is really the return to sovereignty," says Litefoot.

The Stoney Nakoda Nation's leaders are speaking about the culture and history that brought them to today and are making choices to ensure a prosperous tomorrow. The hiring of new CEO Greg Varricchio in the fall of 2009, marked the return to "Self-Sustainability." After inheriting a fiscally dysfunctional administration he quickly agreed with Chiefs and Councils' assessment that the disconnect in the system was due to the omission of traditional practices.

"The nations weren't being managed in Stoney fashion," Varricchio said. "We set about integrating their culture in every aspect of governing and community and economic development. Sustainability, economic and cultural, begins with the guarantee of individual support. To heal a nation you must see issues from their perspective and utilize their traditional approach."

In the words of Bearspaw Elder Virgle Stephens, "To understand a culture you have to use their language. When you understand the language you can begin to understand the nation and its needs."

Nonetheless, the magnitude of the blessings born from ancient spiritual practices cannot be accurately conveyed within the constraint of mere words. Some of their transforming results, however, can. After reestablishing traditional Sundances, pipe ceremonies, smudgings, and prayer as key part of governing, the Stoney Nakoda Nation experienced immediate and dramatic results.

Prayer and pipe ceremonies were held to address the plight of approximately 900 people reliant on income support. Directly following this effort by Chiefs and administration one third of those people signed up to work.

"Prayer was given to us by the Great Creator and First Nations turn to that for spiritual guidance," says Chief Clifford Poucette of the Westley First Nation. "Any ceremony, event, or meeting is opened with prayer. It guides our decisions to initiate change. It's powerful medicine. Since we've been employing our pipe ceremonies in administration the outcome has been positive."

"When they were taking over our lands they took everything from us. Everything but our prayer pipes because they knew their power," added Chief Bruce Labelle of Chiniki First Nation. "To this day we survive and we will be here for the next thousand years because we rely on prayer and our connection to our creator."

Applying the wisdom of the past with the plight of the present has not only begun to heal issues previously deemed insurmountable, it has also fortified all three Stoney Nations on a path of independence.

"We stand together, work together, and never put our colleges down," added Elder Stephens. "When we reestablish these traditional ways we forge unity."

This mindfulness, combined with faith, hope, love, and understanding, is the teaching of the elders. Although mainstream society may still view First Nations people in a general negative light, the time to change that through the rebirth of original power has arrived.

"We have good things to offer, but we must take ownership of who we are before we can share it," says Chief Bearspaw.

In the end Litefoot believes, "it's up to each individual to seek the Creator out and understand there is something tailored specifically for them. When you can remind people of that and bring them to it the benefit is beyond words.

"When you're aware of the power of the Creator you can't be anything other than humbled by it and in awe of it."

The world is out of balance, too much technology unguarded by wisdom and not enough spirituality. And so awakens the prophecy that the teachings being handed down are sacred and crucial to restoring the world's balance.

"That's what the elders and my father would say," explains John Snow Jr. "That the time is coming to impart this knowledge and our elders today are spiritual guides here to help with all things, including our survival.

"We have to return to our traditional ways, be careful with what we say and do, be respectful of Mother Earth and of all life, and consider not only this life but the next–the things we do not yet see or understand.

"We are servants waiting to be called upon."

These are the voices whispering wisdom, these are the methods of healing, this is the time to reclaim a great spirit.

Listen. Practice. Pray.

"Our power, our strength comes through our prayers by asking first for guidance from the Great Creator." – Wesley Elder Bill Wesley

Anticipating the complexities of a new millennium caught between that which threatens our existence and the potentially limitless opportunities to expand as a people, Litefoot answers the call and offers a keystone to the center of self and the connection to the Great Creator for all who seek *The Medicine of Prayer*.

STONEY·TRIBAL
ADMINISTRATION

Introduction

"What would you begin to do, if you knew anything was possible?
Well know this: All things are possible with the Creator."

Pray. That's what I did when I started on this road nineteen years ago. And pray is what I continue to do now that my journey has taken me to places I had never dreamed. Who ever heard of a Cherokee rap artist? No one had heard of such a thing back in 1991. But since then, I have learned that all things are indeed possible with the Creator. I've had the blessing of being able to perform for my people on reservations throughout North America. The blessing has been mine to reach out to young people with positive messages of the spirit; to create a record label and release eleven albums; to travel the world and act in major motion pictures and network television. It has been my humble honor to have the lyrics to my music used to teach both high school and college level students, throughout the United States and as far away as Germany, about historical and contemporary Native American issues. All this and so much more has been the blessing of constant prayer. Whenever I travel, a question I'm asked is this: "Litefoot, how did you get started?" I tell them, first, I prayed.

My relationship with the Creator through prayer has been my teacher, my guide, my comfort. It has been my medicine and...my challenge. Because, let's be honest...the ego doesn't always want to do what the Creator asks...it is not an easy road. But it is the only road to fulfillment.

The Medicine of Prayer is what heals and gives enough strength to the spirit to accomplish anything in this world.

As I have traveled from reservation to reservation throughout North America, as well as non-Native communities around the world, I see the same thing over and over again. So many people are ailing in their spirit. So much time is spent searching for happiness, searching for that something to ease restless hearts. And people try many different means to remedy this internal sickness of why they can't be content. The search for the cure happens in a wide variety of familiar and tragic ways. You know what I'm talking about. The usual suspects we hear about all the time – drinking, violence, drugs, sex – all the addictions. But the illness never goes away.

Now, you know when you're physically ill you need medicine and healing. But there's a tendency to forget that it's not just the body that needs healing – we also need to take care of our spirits. I can truthfully say, from the authority of my own experience, that the only thing that will truly cure the discontent that eats away at the spirit is to build a relationship with the Creator. To do this, we need to communicate. And the way in which we communicate with the Creator is through our prayer. Prayer has healed my spirit and guided my path. *The Medicine of Prayer* has provided any and everything of value in my life.

In my journey, as I've put my feet on just about every reservation in the United States of America, and as I've sat with our people, I continue to hear the things that our people desire, the things that our people want: the ways that our ancestors knew, the things that our ancestors knew as a way of life – that fulfillment on a day to day basis. We want it for our young people. But I can count on one hand the number of times I've seen anyone stand up in front of our people on any reservation in North America and encourage our people without hesitation to pray as a priority in Indian Country.

Several years ago, a tribal leader of a reservation told me that they knew how to fix the problems they were having with the young people and drugs. They were going to go all out and bring tradition back to the kids. And I said, you know, teaching young people about the gifts of the Creator -- the traditional ways, is a good thing. But think about this. If you give the people the gifts of the Creator and they don't know the Creator, you haven't given them anything. They can sing the songs, but if they don't know the Creator then the songs don't mean a whole lot. You can teach them to speak their Native language or how to make those drums, but if they don't know the Creator it won't solve anything.

We can teach our children all day long about "tradition and culture," but it is in vain if we don't put the Creator first before all the gifts of the Creator. Because when our young people know the Creator and they sing songs at the drum, then it will have power. When you put the Creator first and express your traditions, then the culture will have meaning. Give the people, especially our young people, the Creator first in all things. In this way, you feed the spirit, which has been starving.

Often, when I speak with the youth across the country, I ask them what might at first glance, be considered a silly question. I ask, "Has anybody ever heard of NASA just putting a couple of space suits into the space shuttle and sending it up? No astronaut, just the empty suit?" No, we've never heard of that, they respond. I continue, saying: "You know, as valuable as that space suit is, it's worthless out in space without a trained, healthy astronaut inside of it." And then I ask them: "How valuable is the human body?" I tell them that studies have been done to determine the value of a person's arm or a finger in terms of insurance. It's millions of dollars. Even without insurance estimates, we instinctively understand the value of our bodies. We take great care of them. How many countless hours are spent educating, washing, toning, feeding, exercising, and decorating our bodies? The money spent on cosmetics alone is staggering. But what we don't recognize is that our body is just the suit...it's our human suit. It's the suit that our spirit needs in order to exist on Earth. And like a space suit, it needs an "astronaut" in it to reach its potential. The Creator has put something inside our human suit to fulfill our purpose. Our spirit. Have you nourished your spirit? Have you exercised your spirit? Have you communicated with your spirit?

Our ancestors knew that caring for the spirit was a priority over caring for the flesh. That's why during some of our sacred ceremonies, when we sacrifice ourselves in a physical manner, we don't worry about the flesh. When our ancestors went out to battle, they didn't worry about the body. Our people didn't put armor on. They didn't go find the thickest trees and skin the bark off them and put it all over the body. As a matter of fact, if anything, our people stripped down to barely anything. But one thing our ancestors did do, was take care of their medicine and their relationship with the Creator before stepping one foot on that battlefield. Yet today, all that we seem to do is try to give our young people armor. How foolish have we become?

Prayer is the ultimate way to keep your spirit in good health and to nurture and grow your purpose on this Earth. It's the tangible intangible. It is the only armor we need.

Pray. This is a word that has so many different meanings to each one of us. To some it means to bend your knees or your backs in supplication. To others it means to be still and turn within. Yet others pray by appreciating nature – a sunrise, a bird in flight or the waves of the ocean. Whatever prayer means to you, do that.

Because what is common in all these things is the search for a connection to a higher power -- guidance, peace, answers, help and healing. This is what I call *The Medicine of Prayer*.

How do I know the truth of all this? How can I be certain that prayer is a viable solution to the ills we face in life? I can only tell you that the power of *The Medicine of Prayer* has been and continues to be the story of my life.

~ Part One ~
In a Humble Way

"Grandfather, Give me strength
In a humble way, Hear my prayers
Make me safe, Give me strength
In my heart, Hear my soul" -LF

Chapter One

~ Walk With The Creator ~

"Ask the Creator for what you need and have faith it will come.
But faith without work will reap you nothing.
Pray and go hard every day!"

Sept. 11, 1981 – It was my 13th birthday. In my mother's tradition, this was a very important time. In her family, which descends from the Chichimeca Indians of Mexico, when a son or daughter reaches the age of thirteen it is a rite of passage into adulthood. My Mom had planned a party for me at the popular local hangout, Mazzio's Pizza. Those of you from Oklahoma know about Mazzio's. I was looking forward to being with my friends and having a good time. This was the day that would set me off into my manhood.

The way my younger sister tells the story, my Mom was a little hesitant about what she wanted to write on my birthday cake. Should it be a typical young man theme, like football? Or should she go with her first choice, which was something spiritual? She was worried that it might bother me with all the other kids there. My sister responded as our mother had taught us – you can never go wrong with something you feel spiritually led to do, whether his friends liked it or not.

And so, at this popular pizza parlor, with all my jock 12 and 13 year old friends acting out as boys do, my Mom presents me with a birthday cake with a Bible verse on top: Jeremiah 29:11 – *"For I know the plans that I have for you. They are plans for good and not for evil. To give you a future and a hope."*

My first reaction was: "Mom…can't I just have a cake and it not be something profound?" She could see that I wasn't completely comfortable, but she then said something that settled me. "This is what I claim for you." I never forgot that. Though I was embarrassed then, I appreciate her now for her courage in being so strong in her faith – it completely shaped me and grew my belief. Mom taught me that my walk in life could only be fulfilled when it is a walk with the Creator as my guide. Although both my parents are strong in their spirit, it was from my mother that I first came to understand the power of *The Medicine of Prayer*. You could say she was my first spiritual teacher.

Olga O. Pinédo Davis was born in Sacramento, California. Her mother, Paula Pinédo, was a medicine woman born in a village outside the city of Zacatecas in Mexico. My mother tells me how normal and natural it was to find my grandmother praying or talking aloud to get rid of negative energies. How her mother would pin a small medicine pouch to the inside of her blouse everyday as she sent her off to school. This gentle, sweet spirited woman died a week before I was born. My mother was determined to have her spirit carry on in me and so she blessed me by naming me Gary, after my father, and Paul after my grandmother, Paula. And Mom insisted that both names would be spoken, so that I was never just called Gary. To this day, I am Gary Paul, so that my grandmother's spirit would always be in our awareness.

Mom spoke of spirituality in Christian terms. As with the history of many of our people, she was the product of a Catholic upbringing originally put upon the Chichimeca people by the Spaniards. As she grew older she had questions and broke from that strict Catholic doctrine and began to look toward Christianity in a non-denominational fashion. In no way was I taught to, nor do I discount the teachings of Christianity, but I believe the Creator has given us unique ways to express ourselves spiritually. By the time I became old enough to have my understanding of things, I chose to develop and practice my faith in the Creator by taking part in the traditional ways of my ancestors.

My family is a prime example of the result of colonization and the oppression that comes with it: loss of culture and the ongoing struggle to reclaim that culture; of being put upon as a people, by force, to implement the imposing group's culture over your own, whether you like it or not, in the pursuit of whatever agenda the imposing party has. The after effects of that last from generation to generation. You begin to understand how religion is used to control people. For instance, it is a Christian teaching that when two or more are gathered in the name of God, so too is the presence of God. But, nowhere does it say in the Bible, you have to go to church. The Bible says you should congregate with those who believe as you do. The structures of religion that have been created by men have been used so often, and specifically in the history of the Native people in North America, as a means of control and oppression. That is not what I think the Creator wants as the end result of our relationship with him – to feel oppressed, controlled or that there is only one set way to develop your spiritual relationship with Grandfather.

There were times when my mother and I would have deep conversations about prayer and referring to God as the "Creator"; it was clear to me that the Creator has many, many names, in many tongues. I sometimes call him Grandfather, as he is our oldest relative and teacher -- He knows all. Our people have many names for Him, but no matter what name we call Him, it's all the same. There is only one God.

There are numerous references in the Bible and many theological books that we should find freedom through our relationship with the Creator – not chains and things that bind us. We should find the loosing of all things that restrict or control us. If you do it the other way, where people feel oppressed, you stifle the growth of someone's spiritual life and ultimately achieve a negative end result, even though your intentions were good. We should find our place within the infinite and not in the finite bounds of a person. It didn't make sense to me to take refuge in the religion of men, who have a set and very defined beginning and end. But rather, to put the Creator first, which has no beginning or end. The more we focus on our relationship with the Creator and the pureness of that direct relationship, the more we understand, on a continuous basis, a pureness and a power as we've never known it. You begin to truly understand that the water that flows from the river that is the Creator is the sweetest thing you've ever tasted. This is the sweetness of *The Medicine of Prayer*.

I believe my mother got me into Christian schools in order to know the teachings of Christianity and to build an understanding of spirituality. Later, I would then take those understandings and worship in a way that was more in keeping with who I am as a Native person. When I took those understandings and went to our Cherokee Stomp Dances, the Sweat Lodge, the Sun Dance, Longhouse or Hogan or been blessed to be part of any ceremony, I've been able to pray and appreciate the magnificence of the Creator by understanding that long before me the Creator gave all people a way to worship that was meaningful to them. But I would never say one was better than the other, because they are all of the

Creator. Every way the Creator has given us is a vessel to utilize to communicate with the Creator. They are all the best, because they come from the Creator. My studies of the Bible weren't to discount it, but to have an interpretation of it based on the experiences of my life; to find the truth in it and ultimately see the similarities we all share as children of the Creator, rather than the differences.

And so, my earliest understanding of prayer was from a Christian perspective and the Bible. Tied to that was always my mother, who encouraged me to understand how powerful prayer is and how ready and willing the Creator is to listen and help us.

There is a vivid memory I have of a warm, sunny Oklahoma day. I was about ten years old and my mother decided our lunch would be a picnic in the backyard. She brought out the blanket and food. It was just the two of us. That day, she helped me understand what communicating with the Creator was about. She spoke about how there's always more strength in prayer when people are gathered together and focused on the intention of communicating with the Creator. She told me that I always had the opportunity to speak with the Creator and let Grandfather know what was on my heart. These are the words as I remember them:

"We need to talk to the Creator in the way we would talk to a confidante, a friend or family member. That can be done verbally or without saying a word. It is an expression of your heart. The Creator knows what your intentions are and what your meaning is. In prayer, we come from the most sincere place."

She also encouraged me to be more in a constant state of prayer. This is what we should always be doing rather than only praying on a certain day or a certain time of day. She would say, "There is never a time when the Creator is too busy to hear what you have to say."

Praying is everything you do…it's how you eat your food, put on your clothes, it's how you speak…it's how you hold yourself as you walk in your journey of this life. Prayer is how we look at life; how we hold ourselves in a constant awareness of our connection with the Creator. Being able to stay in your spirit from moment to moment and not get caught up in everything around you, to stay focused, or appreciate all that you've been given, are all prayers.

Although these teachings from my mother have guided me throughout life, it wasn't that, as a kid growing up in Tulsa, Oklahoma I was advertising my relationship with the Creator. Not many kids do. Obviously at that age, discussions of faith and religion weren't the topics of conversation amongst my friends. I was not the most outgoing kid when it came to people who I didn't know outside of my family or close friends. I played sports – football in particular. But I wasn't the one who signed up for the debate team, or school plays or anything that would put me forward in that way.

My mother and father always encouraged me to step forward and to never be ashamed or intimidated, but it took me some time to find out the ways in which I was comfortable doing so. When I was cast in the random elementary or middle school play – I remember being filled with anxiety but I always had the support of my family cheering me on to do my best. And even though I always seemed to rise to the occasion, there was nothing I wanted to do less than speak in front of any group of people. I just didn't feel this was me. The furthest thing from my mind was to think of growing up to speak in front of crowds, much less to be a performer or motivational speaker.

But as early as the age of seven, my Mom would encourage my sister and me to act out in our faith. In other words, to not be ashamed of any way the Creator was impressing upon us of communicating in prayer. This wasn't always easy for me.

There was one evening when I was about nine years old; my younger sister didn't want to sleep alone in her room. My father was working. He always worked hard all the time. He had several of his own businesses, so he'd wake up early and leave before we were awake and he would come home late after we were all in bed. Because of this my sister often wanted my Mom to sleep in her bed. So, being the protective older brother that I was, I volunteered to sleep on the floor, so we'd all be in the same room.

My sister, Angelique, was playing this Christian worship song on the kiddie record player she had in her room and singing before going to bed. She would sing herself to sleep many nights. My mom and my sister kept encouraging me to sing too. I wasn't really singing, just mumbling. I was hesitant to sing out. But my Mom kept encouraging me to sing. She said it wasn't about what anybody else thought; there was no bad or wrong way to communicate with the Creator. So, I started to sing more. We sang the song over and over again.

The more I sang, the more I became lost in my connection with the prayer of the song. After a while, I realized that my Mom and sister had stopped singing. It was only me, laying there on my back, with tears streaming down into my ears. I was so caught up in the song, caught up in my spirit, lost in my communication with the Creator.

It was then that I truly began to understand what my Mom meant when she spoke of the dynamic we develop with the Creator at all times. In the small moments and the big ones, in good times or bad, we should be thankful to the Creator. Every moment, everything we have is a blessing from the Creator. In all that we do, God, the Creator, is involved. I began to see that we could control our circumstances with the way we walk with the Creator – our active faith and our belief shapes who we are, who we become.

When I was twelve, Mom encouraged me to go to a camp the church was putting on. At one evening gathering of the entire camp, there was a man speaking. He pointed out a few of us, and asked us to come and stand in front of everybody. I wasn't so thrilled with this. Again, I didn't like being in front of a lot of people. But I went. We were called to the front because he wanted to express to each of us our spiritual gift. When he got to me, he expressed that I had the spiritual gift of exhortation, which is the ability to lift up others with your words and encourage them to fulfill God's purpose for them on the Earth. To be honest, this didn't have a huge impact on me at the time. But I find it amazing how that declaration would become the focal point of my life in later years.

The spiritual foundation that was laid down by my Mom as she raised me up has supported all of my endeavors. The first time I was asked to utilize my gift of exhortation, I had no idea what I was going to say. All I could do was pray to the Creator to give me the words and to have faith that my prayer would be answered. In my nearly twenty years of public speaking I have never sat down before hand and written out what I was going to say, because it is not what "I" want to say. My prayer is to ask the Creator to tell me what it is that needs to be said and then to have the faith to speak those things.

The bottom line is this…Pray. As my mother said to me, I say to you: when you have your prayers, and when you're strong in your prayers there's not anything on this Earth that you can't do or anyone who can stop you. Every single one of us was put here on this Earth to do something.

Now, we often have things that we think we want to do. For instance, I thought I wanted to be a professional football player. But the truth is, there is a difference between what we "want" to do and what we were "born" to do. And the sooner that we come to an understanding of that, the sooner we'll be blessed on this Earth and begin blessing other people.

In my talks, I always tell people: "Don't do what YOU want to do. Find out what the CREATOR has for you to do and you will be fulfilled and happy."

Realize that you've been put here on this Earth to do something...find it and then do it. Your prayers will guide you to what that is. Your prayers will give you your path, your destiny so that you will be fulfilled. Education is a good, good thing. But...it will never give you that. Sports are wonderful, but it will never give you that. I don't care if you make a billion dollars and you're the first person from your community to play in the NBA...even with all of that it's still possible to be miserable. Those accomplishments alone won't bring you fulfillment. You truly should look to what the Creator put you on this Earth to do first. You have a path on this Earth that you were born to walk. If you have the faith to go forward, you will be fulfilled in ways you cannot imagine.

My mother's prayer for me when I reached the age of thirteen carried with it the power of her faith, her love and her complete trust in the Creator. She made a claim for me with the Creator and it is a blessing to live my life in a humble way to honor it.

Chapter Two

- Elders and Ancestors -

"Those that walked before, still in spirit here;
They're reaching out to you – go on - take that hand."

When I was growing up the Native population of Tulsa wasn't large enough to garner a high profile presence or voice in the city. Most Native folks seemed to hang in the periphery, living in the adjoining towns on the outskirts of the city. The Davis family, headed by my grandparents, was no different. This was before Indian Gaming became the billion dollar industry it is today. The Cherokee, Muscogee-Creek and Osage tribes had yet to become the region wide entertainment draw that casino gaming would make them in Tulsa decades later.

When I was a child in the early 1970's, it seemed Native people were nearly invisible to the mainstream population of Tulsa short of the obligatory media coverage given to the Tulsa Powwow or other random press that Native people or tribes would sporadically receive. Through the scattered placement of our Native people all over Oklahoma, we had become isolated and relegated to tiny tribal "islands" in remote areas spread all over the State. The fight for each tribe to survive had for the most part led to a "go for self" political posturing thus further eliminating the hope of ever unifying our people into a strong, cohesive and present voice in Oklahoma.

Many tribes in Oklahoma have been able to make great strides in the areas of economic development and tribal infrastructure.

However, I am sure that many people would agree today that we haven't come that far from the days I remember as a child. As tribal nations, we are still, for the most part, separate tribal islands working independently and often against each other in the grander scope of advancement as a collective.

Somewhere in the middle of this quagmire is the history of my family. It is a shared history of forced removal from our Cherokee homelands in Georgia and Eastern Tennessee via the infamous Trail of Tears, which culminated years later into a struggle to survive in a new land. My ancestors spent their lives grasping for ways to ensure the prosperity of future members of the Davis family – a life also experienced by the thousands of other survivors. I won't venture into the complex historical aspects of Cherokee history and how it impacted our ending up in Oklahoma. The short of it is our Cherokee people had originally been designated lands in the northeastern and south central portions of Oklahoma, the latter widely known as the "Cherokee Strip."

The Cherokee Strip was sold by our nation for $8.5 million dollars and on September 16, 1893, the "Cherokee Strip Land Run" became the largest land run in the history of the United States, opening nearly seven million acres of land to non-Native settlement. The lands of the Cherokee Nation of Oklahoma were reduced to a checkerboard of land claims spread throughout several counties in northeastern Oklahoma.

My great-grandfather, Jess Davis, lived in a house that was basically a hodgepodge of tin siding and wood, slapped together on land allotted by the Cherokee tribe to the Davis family, located near Claremore in Oklahoma. There was a wood-burning stove in the middle of the house and a well and outhouse in the back.

My grandfather, Roy Leo Davis, was born on this land. He was the oldest of his brothers and one sister and was responsible, for the most part, in rearing them. His father, Jess Davis, dealt with daily life in Oklahoma by looking for work where he could find it. Unfortunately, he also did his fair share of finding the bottom of too many bottles of liquor. My grandfather referred to his father simply as the "Old Man."

From my memories as a child, I have a clear vision of the Old Man sitting in a rocking chair in front of his house. He didn't talk much and it kind of always seemed like he was perturbed at something. He was a thin, frail man with thick black-rimmed glasses – he had a bad eye that scared me a little, and he didn't have all of his teeth and usually wore a cowboy hat. When my dad would bring us to Claremore from Tulsa, my great-grandfather would gesture for us to come over and pat us on the back. I never got the impression that my grandfather and father had a very warm nor emotional kind of relationship with the Old Man. I never saw much in the way of compassion between them. Maybe I was just too young to know anything different.

Now, as an adult and a father, I understand the dysfunction within my family – detachment of compassion – a detachment within the family unit because of survival tactics that had been ingrained in our people because of circumstances that were just too overwhelming to contemplate and accept. In my great-grandfather's generation, the evolution of the Davis family had only called for survival. The resulting deterioration of family bonds and relationships was just one of the many casualties of the United States' war against the Cherokee family – a war that lasted long after the final shots had been fired and forced relocation had been completed.

My father had a lot of mixed emotions towards the Old Man. This was due to the stories from family members that he heard growing up. Stories about the harsh ways the Old Man treated my grandfather and the punishment he would receive which came, all too often, when the Old Man was drunk. My grandfather never talked about that.

In the generation with my father and me, we have worked hard to have a better father-son relationship than what my grandfather had with the Old Man. I have definitely changed it with my sons, letting them know that I love them as many times as possible each day and to hug them so they can feel the love I have for them. I never saw this compassion exhibited between my grandfather and his father. It must have hurt my grandfather and left a hollow inside of him. I will never know the answer to that. I wasn't old enough or was unable to understand things clearly enough when he was alive to be able to form those types of questions to ask him. But it does give me even more respect for my grandfather now, because I did see him hug my father and tell him he loved him. He broke the cycle of detachment of compassion so that, in turn, my father did the same with me.

Therefore, one of the greatest teachers in my life -- which includes my mother and my father -- would have to be my grandfather, Pop. A lot of what carries me today and a lot of who it is that I am today comes from talks with my grandfather -- just hours on end spending time with him. Pop was such a gentle spirit. He had a simple but clear understanding of life. He used to tell me that hard work would give you a hard day's pay. And he truly believed in doing the right thing. Pop was a pretty quiet man. If he was having a bad day you wouldn't really know it. I felt comforted just being in his presence. I realize now that the times spent with him, doing what might be considered mundane actions, like weeding the garden, were the times I was being taught the traditional way of living each moment in prayer, despite the challenges imposed by modern society.

Pop worked hard his whole life as a mechanic and manual laborer to give his children a better chance at the "American Dream." Because of the experiences my family endured, I have always felt it inherently wrong, and against the teachings of the Creator, for one group of people to cause by force or ultimatum another group of people to abandon their way of life in order to adopt another. This was exactly the situation that the Davis family, and tens of thousands of other Native families were faced with throughout the United States. There was no way around it or under it. Colonization was not wished for by the indigenous nations of the America's nor was it readily accepted. But it was a reality in which thousands of tribal nations had no choice, other than to deal with the inevitable in the best way they could.

So my grandfather worked relentlessly to provide a better way for his family. I feel his take on life resolved to a simple mantra: "You know who you are, grow up, work hard and provide for your family and you never quit." Two weeks after my father was born at the Claremore Indian Hospital in 1942, my grandfather loaded up his family and in the heat of July, set out on Highway 66 to California with the promise of opportunity and work out west.

This was during an era when decision makers in Washington, D.C. encouraged Native people to move to larger cities throughout the country as part of a new form of "Indian relocation" which promised jobs and a new beginning. In all actuality, the U.S. government was probably far less concerned about the betterment of Native people and providing us with opportunity and more focused on the idea of assimilating away our Native blood lines via their policy of integration. Many of my grandfather's brothers soon followed him out west. Pop stayed in California long enough to raise his two sons, and see my Dad marry and begin his own family. My sister and I were both born out west. However, though

Pop felt the move to California changed his perception of the world and gave him a broader view of possibilities, years later he and all his brothers eventually moved back to the family land in Oklahoma.

When I was four years old my Dad had a dream that led him to return home from California. The vision in his dream was of hands held out to him, reaching out to him to come back home. There is a sculpture at Oral Roberts University in Tulsa of huge bronze hands clasped together in prayer. My father would later say that was the closest thing to what he saw in his dream, even though that sculpture had not yet been built when he had his dream. And so, because of my father's vision, he moved our family back to Tulsa.

My formative years in Tulsa were filled with great memories of being outdoors and playing all kinds of games with my neighborhood friends. In elementary school I would occasionally get in fights when people would make comments because I didn't look exactly like everybody else. My eyes were just a bit too oval and set me apart from the other kids. There was a particular incident in 7th grade when a kid in the school cafeteria kept on about me being Asian, complete with very stereotypical mimicking. I tried to ignore him, but as I was about to sit down he knocked my lunch tray on me. I ended up going to the principal's office for defending myself. But for the most part, I just learned to tolerate the ignorance of other kids.

During this time, I just couldn't wait to get over to my grandparent's house on the weekend and spend time with them. I would tell my grandfather about how some of the other kids behaved towards me. One thing he used to say: "Don't start a fight. Let the other guy throw the first punch, but then you end it." Looking back on these times, I realize I was learning to be a man. And my Pop set the standard high.

Pop was a self-taught man and I believe he could build anything and fix almost anything too. All he learned in his life he taught himself and he used that to make a living for his brothers and sister and then his own family. He was an excellent mechanic and could take apart a car engine and reassemble it with ease. He could build intricate pulley systems and later used this knowledge to start his own tow truck company and manufacture his own lifts and cranes for use with his fleet of auto wreckers. He was an outstanding carpenter and always enjoyed working construction. He was on several occasions offered the opportunity to become a construction foreman or supervisor but he always declined. There were other things in life that he wanted to make time for and I think he knew that accepting a management position would not allow him the time to do the things he loved to do, like work in the garden or go fishing with his grandson.

Pop was not physically a large man and stood a slim 5 feet 8 inches tall. But he was as solid as steel and all one need do to experience that was to shake his hand. My grandfather treated people how he wanted to be treated and even though he did not always get that respect in return he never let the world jade him. I recall plenty of times when I would get so frustrated as a young boy at people who Pop would be talking to and in mid sentence they would just turn and walk off as if they didn't respect him enough to let him finish his sentence. Pop would still be talking but then turn his focus to me to finish his thought. That used to infuriate me.

Another time we went to a local ice cream store in Claremore and the white lady at the counter looked at Pop and asked in real slow broken English "What...Kind...Ice... Cream...You...Want." I was mystified as to why this lady was talking to him in this manner. I thought maybe she had a disability or a problem speaking. Pop replied and clearly said, "I would like a scoop of strawberry and my grandson would like a scoop of chocolate." She looked immediately embarrassed and turned to fill the order. Pop looked at me and I realized she must have thought that because he was an "Indian" he couldn't speak or understand English very well. This made me very upset.

The times that I have experienced racism in my own life or when I have been witness to other people's blatant ignorance, I always recall Pop and how he handled those moments in his life. He would never sink to the level of those who were ignorant toward him. He refused to do so. He never let people's lack of compassion change his nature and he taught me many valuable lessons by watching his example.

Pop and I would talk while we worked in his garden till dark. Afterwards we'd have dinner and then talk for many more hours out on his patio. I remember the ice-cold 12oz. glass bottles of Pepsi that I would nurse while the hours passed listening to my Pop and grandmother's conversations. Occasionally, the blare of a horn from a train off in the distance interrupted the evening conversation. But mostly, it was the easy cadence of his voice that I remember on those warm Oklahoma nights with the crickets chirping in the background.

Sometimes Pop took me with him when he would go meet "old man" Rabbit who was his friend and a Cherokee painter from Claremore. Pop would sit and talk to him, and I would sit and listen to these two elders speak. Other times we would go out to our family's allotted land outside of Claremore and I would visit my cousins while Pop would visit with his brothers.

My experience as a young Cherokee was more about being around my immediate family rather than that of a larger tribal interaction. A person is not taught to be an "Indian." You learn those things as you're living…from those who are your family.

Now that I am an adult, I recognize that every time my grandfather took me with him to fish, or to hunt or to do anything, he was my teacher. He was teaching me about being "Cherokee" just by being with him, listening to him talk, working with him in the garden – listening to his views on life. I didn't know I was learning to pray, but I know now that those times when I was with my grandfather…that was prayer. The same applies with my parents. That's something you learn through actions. You can't be told how to be a man, you have to be shown.

Pop read the Bible at least 15 times front to back. Sometimes I would come in, he would be sitting there with the television on, but he would be reading the Bible. However he would never force his views of religion upon anyone else. It may have been because of his experience at the boarding school that he attended in north central Oklahoma.

At the beginning of his 6th grade year, he and a younger brother were sent away from their family to Chilocco Indian School. The tragic history of the abuse suffered by Indian children in these schools is all too true. After a few weeks at Chilocco, my Pop had enough. He took his younger brother and sneaked out and somehow traveled the 133 miles, on foot, from the school north of Newkirk, Oklahoma all the way back to our family land outside of Claremore, Oklahoma. After he ran away from Chilocco Indian School, he never again pursued a formal education.

Obviously, because of the United States' history of using religion to exact their will on the Native population, many of our people today have a problem with Christianity. That's what happens when people take spirituality and make it a religion and furthermore abuse it. Humans are imperfect and when we take

27

something pure, the moment we touch it, we have the potential to infect it, even when we don't intend to.

We have to be incredibly delicate in how we handle the spirit. I believe there are many good spiritual teachings, delivered in many different forms that the Creator put here for us on Earth to learn from and to use in our lives. We should open our minds to them and the good that all people have to offer. We shouldn't let the misuse of religion against Native people cause us to turn against good things that may help us. It's not that the essence of religion is wrong, but rather those who used that purity in the wrong way. When we remain open in our heart to see things not as the world views them, but as the Creator intended them to be, we literally open up a whole new world from which we can learn and grow.

There is a story I heard during one of my visits to the Pine Ridge Indian Reservation in South Dakota about when missionaries came to talk to the Lakota war leader, Crazy Horse. At the time, the Lakota were being hunted by the United States government and it was taking a toll on his camp. A priest came to encourage Crazy Horse to know more about Jesus. The priest began to speak to him about who Jesus was. Finally, after the priest was done talking, Crazy Horse nodded his head and told the priest that this Jesus sounded like a good Lakota man.

The life of Crazy Horse has always been an inspiration to me. Once he had received his vision as a young man, he did his best to stick to the path given him by the Creator. He had complete faith in what he had been shown. Because of that faith, he was fearless in battle and walked with confidence in the medicine he carried. He knew his purpose and fulfilled it, even knowing the manner in which he would be called home. Historical accounts of his life speak of his constant state of prayer -- that he would spend little time in the village bragging or boasting of his deeds in battle like the other warriors. Instead, Crazy Horse would spend most of his time alone in the surrounding woods in communion with the Creator. He would return to the village with his spirit replenished and strengthened to again carry forward his purpose. Crazy Horse's way of life continually kept him in a state of prayer and allowed him the strength to manifest the gifts of his vision into reality. He understood that prayer is medicine and allowed his life to be an example from which we could all learn.

The ancestors lived and taught that prayer is everything you do – everything you do is a prayer – it's not a singular action – it's how you live your life.

And just like sometimes when you take medicine, you're told to take it with food? With prayer you have to use faith. And once you begin to step out and practice these things – when you begin to exercise your faith -- you begin to see results. I head coach my eldest son's youth football team. If our team never practiced, I doubt we would be very successful. I constantly remind the team that by giving their all at practice, they will reap the rewards from those efforts on game day. I tell them it is simple, "You will play like you practice." The process is the same with praying.

When we exercise our faith through our prayers, our faith grows as our prayers are answered. One begets the other but they have to be used. It is always amazing to me how many people only pray when they need something and then lose faith in their prayers when they are not answered moments later. Throughout our history, the ancestors not only tell us, but also show us by their actions that prayer strengthens your relationship with the Creator and gives you clarity. Prayer is the strongest medicine there is to cure the disease of discontentment, being miserable, unfulfilled or un-happy. These feelings come upon people when they are without a purpose.

The words of the elders and our ancestors constantly encourage us to remember that the source of our power is and always has been the Creator. There is nothing more important than our relationship with the Creator. In each moment, you always want to be prepared and be sure everything is in order with the Creator.

In these times, however, many people feel that prayer is nice, but not something that could be the foundation of their lives. Because prayer is not something we can put in our hand and hold, most people think it doesn't have any power -- it couldn't be a realistic answer for struggle or to deal with everyday occurrences in our life. Maybe it worked for our ancestors a long time ago, but this is the 21st century. We need 21st century answers.

There is a prophecy left to us by our ancestors, which says that there will come a time of turmoil on the Earth. The winged will come to warn the people that they are not acting in accordance with the ways of the Creator and to encourage them to humble themselves to Grandfather. If they do not listen, then the four-legged will walk this Earth and remind the people and warn them. And if they still pay no mind to these messengers, the Creator will send the two-legged messengers in order to speak directly to people in their language so there can be no misunderstandings and that their ears can hear the message of the Creator encouraging them to return to compassion and righteousness. If we choose to remember the ways of the Creator, compassion and abundance will be shown to us. But those people of Mother Earth who still refuse to listen, the Creator will move upon the Earth and cleanse it of all unrighteousness.

I believe that we are living in the time of the two-legged moving on the Earth and spreading the Creator's message. I believe that throughout the world different people from different walks of life are speaking and saying: "Humble yourselves to the

Creator and teach your children to pray by remembering to pray yourselves." Remember, you can't be "told" how to "be" - you must be "shown" how to be. Through our prayers we are able to be examples of strength to others and help them come closer to that which gives them purpose. The Creator.

Today, people are getting their encouragement from main stream media, living their lives according to what they see on television, read in magazines, watch in movies, etc. And that messaging is so loud and constant that people can't hear what the ancestors are saying anymore. The ancestors have been telling us what time it is. It is time to pray and look to the Creator to become a strong people again. To look to the Creator to become the people that we are intended to be.

We must understand that we have all been born to this Earth for a reason. No one on Earth is here for no reason. Through our prayers we'll be shown what it is that we are supposed to do with the gift that is our life. Our life then literally becomes a real time example to everyone with whom we come in contact as to the power of the Creator and the unlimited possibilities that come with connecting to our purpose. In discovering our purpose we also discover that we've been given all the tools necessary to accomplish everything that we have been born to do.

This is why I always encourage people to recognize the difference between what you want to do and what you have been BORN to do. Then you will see that you are able to accomplish with ease what others spend a lifetime attempting to do. When you find the purpose for which you have been born to this Earth, you can stop surviving and start living!

Life comes through the Creator and prayer is how you communicate with the Creator. Prayer is the way you strengthen and feed your spirit. Far too many people have given up on themselves and their communities because they see no hope in things ever changing. In over two decades of traveling reservation to reservation throughout Indian Country, I've seen so many people who seem to feel that there is just no point in fighting for their purpose. They feel their life has none. I've seen people who speak of the old ways as if the Creator is not capable of providing us NEW ways to heal and help ourselves.

Yet, I have never seen in all my travels any problem, sickness or obstacle bigger than the Creator. There is nothing bigger than the Creator and the power of prayer.

The Medicine of Prayer means first coming to an understanding of your own innate sincerity and to also discern in that sincerity truly what it is you need and not what you merely want -- to understand the power of your thoughts and intention so that you use them in a responsible way.

The more that you see prayers answered and you begin to understand the power of prayer, you learn to be careful what you pray for. You come to know that the Creator really is listening to us. And you don't have to speak something out loud to be heard. It's just as important to be aware of your thoughts. The Creator knows the condition of your heart. Understanding this, you begin to develop more truthfulness in your own self. Because you can tell people anything, but the Creator knows where you truly are.

Having a relationship with the Creator allows you to really humble yourself. When you have to recognize your condition, it immediately allows you to remove all the pretense and become focused on moving forward from where you truly are. I believe that's what the Creator wants – to take us from the place where we are and build us into who He wants us to be. But we each must first be humble and accept who we are and where we are so that we don't start building from a false place. When you begin to humble yourself you become like moldable clay. Then the Creator can mold you in ways you could never do yourself, shaping you into the person you were born to be. You become the change that you so wish to see in others. My grandfather believed that "All things are possible through the Creator."

Pop was right!

Chapter Three

~ Lessons ~

"Let the Creator fight your battles! Instead of responding to negativity, hatred, jealousy & opposition directly-pray instead! Everyday we learn."

Pray for what you need, not for what you want. This can mean many different things to many people. So often we think of prayer as a way to get material things. And we can get pretty specific about it, too. For instance, praying for a particular kind of car, or that your child gets all A's and a scholarship to your favorite college. You can debate that these are needed things. A car is needed to get to work, or that GPA is necessary to get into that particular university. But why limit the gifts of the Creator? Before we can even put into words what we think we want, we should realize that our Creator has already planned out all the days of our lives. We should know that regardless of how difficult things get for us, the Creator already knows best what we need and has prepared a way for our prayers to be answered.

What do we need? We need abundant faith in the Creator to show us our path and our purpose. It ALL begins there. Of course, getting to work is important. But maybe you don't need a car. Maybe you need to take up your colleague's offer to carpool, because there is some wisdom for the two of you to share or you may need to learn the lesson of being humble and accepting a gift when it's offered. And there's no question getting straight A's can be beneficial. But how can you be certain that college is the path for your child? What could be better than to pray for the Creator to show you and your child what you need to fulfill the purpose for which the Creator put you here on this Earth? As the Creator walks with you on your path and guides you, you grow stronger each day and begin to know first hand the power of your prayers. Importantly, by the life you lead, you will, without even trying, teach others…including your children, *The Medicine of Prayer*.

Throughout my childhood, I was blessed to learn about *The Medicine of Prayer* from my parents and grandparents. No matter what got thrown at them, they never stopped. And that was something that I had to learn. It was as I walked through my teen years that I experienced the lesson of how to pray for what it was I truly needed.

During my childhood my father worked to build a good life for his family. He was and is a man who created opportunities. He would learn how a business was run, then build a business on his own. Starting from the ground up, he had several enterprises going while I was growing up: a car lot, an auto garage and a construction company. He often hired family members and he contributed to the community, helping to build a church through the construction business.

In time for my dad's 40th birthday, we moved into a new home that he had built. All the years it had taken to build up his businesses, my dad had never taken a vacation. Now that things were going well, he decided to give us the kind of family vacation we'd never had. It was the summer before I began 9th grade at Eastwood Baptist School in Tulsa, OK. My sister had celebrated her coming of age 13th birthday in the new house. My Dad was determined to give us the best of family vacations. He rented an RV and mapped out a trip that would have us travel to the Grand Canyon, out to California, the works.

For several months, Dad had given jobs at his business to his older brother, who had been let go at his job. And since this had been working out, Dad felt it was a good time for our trip since he could leave the reins of the business with my uncle.

In those days there was no instant communication systems like we have today. No text messaging, emails and cell phones. My father had no way of knowing that in the two weeks he was away, everything he had built up over fifteen years was about to come cascading down.

My father had told my uncle not to sign any deals, or make any payments during the time he was away. Anything of that nature could wait the two weeks until our return. There was a roof being installed at one of my fathers' construction sites which was completed during our vacation and my uncle made the decision to pay them by going to the bank and turning over the titles of all the cars on the lot for cash. He then paid the roofing company for putting on a metal roof, without knowing that the installation of the roof was totally faulty. In fact, they had put the materials on upside down. Upon our return we found that my uncle had put my father's businesses completely in debt without any means to repay the bank for the loans they made on the car titles. My Dad tried to regroup, but within a year everything had been mortgaged. We lost the garage, the construction company, the car lot and the home my father had just built for us. There was no salvaging the relationship between my dad and uncle either. It's been more than twenty-five years now, and the brothers don't speak to this day.

In the months after this calamity, my father worked harder than ever to save his businesses. I wanted to do whatever I could to help out – I was old enough to get a job. But my mother insisted that I stay in school – that was my job, to get an education. But compared with what was happening in my life, school seemed trivial. My father had a vision that brought him back to Oklahoma from where he grew up in California. He'd created a good life for us and now we were learning the lesson of what was real – what was of value.

As I look back on this time, I look back with great respect for my parents. This could have been a tragic turning point – an opportunity to give up. My parents had an unwillingness to accept that their circumstance would determine their response in a negative way. Falling into despair just wasn't an option. I know it was a blessing that they had fighting spirits. There was no sense of giving up. There was no sense that these circumstances would be our permanent lot in life. Even as the months passed and the struggle became more difficult, still my parents held to their faith and pushed forward.

As I began my sophomore year of high school my entire world was about to be irrevocably altered. Hard as he tried throughout the past year, my Dad was unable to recover his businesses. That fall and winter, things came to a head. As the holiday season drew near, Mom did her best to ensure we had a happy Christmas. There was clearly no money for gifts, but she went to one of the church centers and got a gift for my sister and me. The generic gift tags were still on them that showed if it was a gift for a boy or girl and the age range. I don't remember what mine was, but my sister still has hers – a radio. And though Mom tried to shield us from the news, it was hard not to know when the Sheriff came and put the eviction notice on the door the day after Christmas. But in the spirit of the season, the Sheriff allowed us to stay until after the New Year.

Needless to say, the upheaval took a severe toll on our family. With everything crashing down around me, it would have been easy to give up, or give in to the unfairness of life. The usual avenues were available to me to ease the frustration. Alcohol or drugs, any number of petty criminal activities could have eased the burden of being evicted, having everything taken away. And yet, there was also another choice.

Through *The Medicine of Prayer*, you can trust that there are teachings in everything that happens. Through your prayers you are able focus on understanding the teaching instead of the roar of the struggles. When you have the confidence that the Creator is with you and that your life has purpose and focus, you are able to stay present and respond to the situation, not react. When you know the truth of prayer and how powerful that you are through the utilization of your prayers, then you can put all things in perspective – in proper context and better find the teachings you are meant to receive.

Even during this time, my Mom still held to and expressed the belief to be grateful. Expressing gratitude is prayer. To thank the Creator for all that you have been given says to the Creator: "I'm not forgetting the blessings you've already brought my way." Especially in challenging times it is important to replenish the cycle that continues to nourish, guide, motivate and propel you on this journey of your life. This is done through grateful prayer. For those who don't learn these things, it just seems to be one more hardship that has no answer. But when you understand how to work within it, you realize that you have the ability to choose how you respond to these things. Continued momentum is dependent on how you respond. You always have a choice in how you deal with problems and obstacles.

Because my parents refused to fall into the trap of using alcohol to ease their pain, it wasn't an option for me. Long ago, my parents had made the choice of not following in the footsteps of some family members who were drinkers. There was simply no time for it. We were in a sinkhole in the sand and doing everything to stay afloat. It didn't make sense to stop and go drinking. In fact, I've never seen my dad drunk in my whole life. Neither of my parents were big drinkers, though they might have a glass of wine or an occasional beer.

I learned from family stories that my grandfather and his brothers had definitely had a problem with drinking. What solved my grandfather's drinking was my grandmother. One day when she came home, he was drunk. She packed up and that was it. She basically left, telling him that she was not going to deal with him drinking. Apparently he got a bad temper once he was drunk. Her leaving cleared it for him. He did relapse once in my memory. It was in their little house in Claremore. My sister and I were young, but one day my grandmother got us together and took us to a hotel. She told us she was checking in to the hotel for the weekend so that we could go swimming. The next day I remember my grandfather showing up to the hotel and that was the last time he ever got drunk. After that, the only time I saw my grandfather drink was if he got a bit of a cold he'd take a swig of apricot brandy. He kept it in the refrigerator. That same bottle was in there for years and never made it below half full.

At the time of us losing everything, being a teen, I wasn't consciously aware of the motivation of why I didn't quit or give in. I was fighting to not get overwhelmed by my circumstances in life. I learned from my parents – you have to keep climbing.

It was during this time that I learned to express myself through writing and poetry. In those days before losing the house, I would sit at my desk and listen to the radio, mostly the classical music station. There were so many thoughts in my head I needed to listen to music that had no words. And as I listened, all my thoughts and prayers would come out on the page. Sometimes they were stories inspired by the passion of the music and the upheaval of my life. Other times they were poems. This was my way of connecting with my spirit, giving it breathing room, giving voice to what was on my heart. Praying.

Now, as I travel to reservations and talk to people, I do understand how dire people's experiences are sometimes – and those circumstances can put you in a mind-frame that things are too big to deal with. I went through that kind of hell myself so I do have compassion for other people when they go through that.

The greatest lesson for me during this time was in understanding that applying *The Medicine of Prayer* into our lives is not so that bad things don't happen. It was and is about utilizing your prayers to sustain you in order to move forward with strength through adversity. As my mother had taught, in the small moments and the big ones, in good times or bad -- be thankful to the Creator. Now was not the time to give up on prayer. Every moment, she taught me, everything we have been given, is a blessing from the Creator. Now was not the time to dwell on the negative, or hold on to regret. Now was the time to seek out the Creator even more. Now was the time to affirm faith and move forward. Through all the confusion, anger, frustration and pain, now was the time for the Creator's medicine.

My parents never lost sight of this. It was their steadfastness in their faith in the midst of everything that happened to our family that taught me this. The only way to overcome life's obstacles and tragedies is to turn to the source of our strength -- the Creator.

Hunting frogs and packing my grandfather's .22 rifle
on our land in Claremore. I was 3 years old.

At my grandparent's house in Claremore at age 11.

At home with Mom, Dad and Angelique in Tulsa.

Mom and I with my 13th birthday cake.

Roy Leo Davis, my grandfather in Oklahoma at age 21.

Jess Davis, My Great Grandfather.

My Grandfather surrounded by his brothers and sisters in Claremore.

My Pop and I at my father's car lot in Tulsa.

Pop and me.

Pop, My Great Grandfather and my Dad eating Christmas dinner at my Pop and Nan's house in Claremore.

My father ran his own businesses and was very successful. I needed to see that as a child in order to know it was possible later on in life.

My family watching football at my Nan and Pop's house.

My father provided very well for his family. My mom always took great care of us kids. This was the calm before the storm.

....

~ Part Two ~

On the Battlefield

"Litefoot, see that road?
That's a warrior's road.
This road is the one chosen for you.
It's a lonely road filled with many hardships
and temptations.
As a warrior you must speak the truth and
fight the good fight.
The Creator watches you.
Your Ancestors guide you.
Never be afraid brother
when your heart is good.
Any day is a good day to die." LF

....

Chapter Four

~ Changes ~

"Never stop, don't quit & rise above all life's challenges.
You really do have the ability to accomplish all you can imagine.
Pray & watch!"

The new year of 1985 did not begin with beautiful fireworks. But there was an explosion of change in my life. Between the ages of fifteen to sixteen everything in my known world changed drastically. It only took one year. Until that point, I lived in a comfortable world, what you might call a middle class, American Dream. Like any other teen, I was looking forward to the experience of high school, playing football, having a social life. I wanted to advance my education, prepare for college. Everything in my life up to that point indicated that this was the path I would take. But things got real serious, real quick. The new house my parents had built was no longer ours and had been foreclosed on by the bank. We were forced to move in with my grandparents in their little house in Claremore. On the one hand, it was wonderful to be with my grandparents. And on the other hand, it was a huge time of tension within my family.

It was frustrating and heartbreaking to see it all go away like smoke. My father, although surely devastated by the events of the past year, continued to push forward through his own anger and sense of betrayal that he experienced from his brother. He found work where he could. My mother had to find work as well. As things began to unravel with my father's businesses and our displacement from our home, the strain on my parent's marriage would prove to be too much: my mother and father separated. And although they split, they still worked hard so that things would be good for their children.

My Mom would always say: *Where there's a will, there's a way.* My mother went to stay with a friend in Tulsa. In search of work, she took a job with a cleaning service called Merry Maids. My mom had always kept our home spotlessly clean and it brought her great joy to keep our household in order. After working at Merry Maids for a short time, my mother started her own housecleaning business. It seems the entrepreneurial spirit has always run strong in my family.

Many of my mother's first clients were friends whom she had known before our world came crashing down. These were very same people my mom went to church with when my father's businesses were flourishing and we still lived in the home my father had built. I know it must have been hard for her to know these people as peers and within a short turn of events was now cleaning their homes. But she taught me to never be ashamed of your circumstances; never be afraid to start over or to move forward. To other people it may not even look like you're moving forward; crawling may be embarrassing to others, but to you it's better than laying there to die.

No matter what got thrown at my parents, they never stopped. And that was something that I had to learn then. My mother personified to me the "whatever it takes" mentality that so many people say they are willing to put in place to achieve their goals, but never actually do. My mother actually did what she had to do in order to achieve her goals and because of this I looked at her with an even greater admiration. She refused to let her pride get in the way.

Soon, she moved into her own apartment and grew her business into one that provided her with a comfortable income and allowed her to take care of not only herself but she was even able to help support me and my sister. My mother's actions during this time in my life taught me to keep moving forward and that the WILL to survive is a powerful WAY to achieve your goals. My mother showed me by example that you can positively change your situation with hard work and perseverance. But it was always clear to me that the strength my mother drew from was her relationship with the Creator.

The Creator was the WILL that gave her a WAY to overcome adversity and keep moving forward. Her walk with the Creator allowed her to be humble yet gave her the self-respect she needed to not let the nature of her work determine who she was as a person. *The Medicine of Prayer* can strengthen your resolve and provide you with focus to overcome all adversity even if it seems that those obstacles are insurmountable. Nothing that you do when you are in compliance with the Creator is demeaning.

When you pray and seek out the Creator, doors open for you and the darkness of your path becomes lit by the light of your faith and hard work. You become confident in moving forward upon your journey and intimately familiar with your guide -- The Creator. When you experience this and know the power of it in your own life, the opinions of others aren't able to distract you from your path, nor influence you to stray off course. The focus you receive and the sensitivity you begin to develop from the Creator are the cornerstones to the foundation of your purpose. You will always rely upon these attributes no matter how high you build your house.

For as long as I can remember, my father has been an example to me that hard work and determination equate to success. These were the attributes I was seeing in my mother as she started her own company. And I also saw these attributes in my father. Growing up, I cannot ever recall seeing my father being a worker for someone else's company. My father was always the owner of his own companies and had people working for him. I pretty much spent my childhood hanging out at his businesses and "helping" him. I am sure that I was often times more in the way than contributing to the success of his companies. But hanging out with my father provided me a real time classroom from which to learn. I sat in with him on meetings at the bank, with suppliers and even with clients. I saw business being done and how he conducted himself in doing business. I also watched how he handled adversity when things didn't go quite as he had planned.

One of the things my father taught me came into play during this time of hardship we were experiencing. Dad always spoke about never being afraid to stand alone or be apart from the norm. He was always a real time example of this to me. I would watch him walk into a meeting and just by using his physical presence, control the room and the direction of the meeting to communicate his thoughts and agenda. He always knew beforehand what he wanted to walk away with from the meeting and he didn't leave until that was accomplished. I watched him execute this important business skill to perfection in multiple settings and on more occasions than I can recall. I would watch different people sit with him in negotiations and initially tell him "no" or that they were "not interested" in whatever he was selling or trying to convey to them. Often, within half an hour I would see him shake their hand and walk away with the sale or the deal closed.

My father taught me to be a better listener than a talker. He would tell me: "Listen to what people say to you, that is the key to communication. If you don't listen to their objections and really understand their position, you will never be able to know what to say to get them to understand yours. Don't argue, communicate." When I saw him deal with an adverse situation, he taught me to be still and not get caught up in everything else that was going on around me. He would say: "The answer to your problem is often right in front of your nose. When you panic or let the problem overwhelm you, it is almost impossible to find the solution and resolve the issue." I learned to respond to problems and not to react to them. All of the life skills my father taught me and the experience I gained by watching and listening to him throughout my youth, are priceless.

Not that my father was without his faults. No man is perfect. There were many times I wished he was able to spend more time with me throwing the ball or being home and not at work till all hours of the night. But, he was doing what he had to do in order to provide the best way he could for our family. It is hard to be two places at once and I am sure my father would have rather been home and spending time with his family, but his businesses did not allow him the time for that. I now understand why he always took me with him to his businesses whenever he could. That is how he was able to be in two places at once. Even though it wasn't ideal "father and son" time, it was time together that he was able to be "present" with me and in my life. I would never replace those days for anything. Because my father made room for me during even the most hectic of business schedules, he was able to be more than just my dad. He became my business teacher and mentor. I owe him much for the abilities and the skills he taught me that I have used in my career to achieve success.

My father also showed me that the burden of responsibility and, more importantly, accountability, is integral to the success of any endeavor. He would say: "It is impossible to be responsible unless you can be held accountable." I apply what he taught me then in each and every day of my adult life.

And so, I started the New Year of 1985 doing my best to be both responsible and accountable. At sixteen years old, I left school and got a job bussing tables. The immediate priority was to help my family...I'd have to finish my sophomore year of high school at a later date. It was a time when I had to learn how to survive, how to understand what was important and getting a real strong dose of life.

It was a critical time for the survival of my family too. I knew education was important and I would be able to complete school eventually, but the moment called for me to pursue a means of giving back to support the family. That was the immediate priority and my response to what life had brought my way.

A friend of my parent's owned two very exclusive restaurants in Tulsa. I went and applied at one of them and got the job. I am sure my mother had something to do with my quick hire. As part of my job, I was required to wear a button down shirt, a necktie and slacks with a long apron to cover the front of my pants. I remember feeling very proud to work at such a nice restaurant and at the proposition of receiving cash tips after each night's work. The pocket money I earned every night allowed me to feel like I was contributing each day toward easing the financial hardship that my family was enduring. I would come home and share my earnings with my family and it made me feel so good. I was able to ease some of the pressure that my parents and grandparents were under to help them buy us all groceries or to pay a bill.

Even though I was beginning to help the family unit and contribute solutions to our dilemma, I was feeling the weight of change. Each night at work I would see tables full of people who were financially and emotionally on the opposite side of the world in which I was living. I would see families eating dinner together who seemed so happy, like they had not a care in the world, while my family was in the midst of being torn apart. My family dinners had been replaced with the free meals that the restaurant graciously offered its employees if you came early for your shift. The restaurant's day old bread was also served with the meal and I don't think I have ever eaten as much bread in my life as I did then. Even though the employee meals wouldn't be considered elaborate dishes, I felt like I was eating better than my family each night. I often felt guilty eating the fettuccini or prime beef with noodles that the chef whipped up. I would think of my family while I stood and ate my food alone in the wait station each evening. They would remain in my thoughts as I made my rounds through the restaurant pouring water or cleaning plates from tables.

Even though I was just a bus boy, I took great pride in my job. I was confident and always polite. I refused to let my job title define me and I would smile at the patrons enjoying their dinner. But many times I would get a smug look in return and instantaneously I felt very much like a lowly bus boy. In those moments I felt pretty alone. But, I would think of my mother who never let people make her feel "less than" and my father who taught me always to be proud of who I was and to never be afraid to stand alone. So as I stood alone doing my job, I refused to let someone else determine who I was or how I should feel about myself or my job.

Something else came to me at that time that helped me tremendously. I recalled my mother always telling me that life is a series of seasons. Much like the actual seasons of Spring, Summer, Fall and Winter, life has seasons too. In life we have times of birth and growth. We have times of abundance, harvest and of reaping the rewards for our efforts. There are even times when things slow down and we have to be patient and wait things out. It never crossed my mind that I would be a busboy forever. I knew that this was but a season in my life.

Many years later, I was eating at a restaurant in Tulsa and saw a Native American teen working as a bus boy. He must have been new to the job as he seemed pretty flustered when pouring water or clearing the plates from a table. As I was watching him, I was instantly taken back to my days of being a bus boy myself. I then saw one of his co-workers get onto him for something he must have done wrong and his shoulders dropped with discouragement. When I finished my meal and was leaving the restaurant I went up to him and introduced myself. I told him to follow his dreams. He recognized who I was from my music and film success and smiled. I then put a hundred dollar bill in his hand and told him I wanted to give him a tip for doing such a great job. I told him to never quit and never give up and to never let others determine how he felt about himself, as I had seen the exchange between him and his co-worker. I told him that I used to be a bus boy and sometimes co-workers and patrons tried to make me feel bad. He couldn't believe I had worked a similar job as his and said, "You were a busboy?" I shook his hand and told him: "This is just a season in your life and a new season is right around the corner for you. Be ready for it."

It felt good to be able to extend that act of compassion and encouragement to him that day. There were many times that I wished someone would have done that for me when I was a bus boy. But, we all have to experience the seasons of our lives to become the people the Creator gave us life to be. We need to learn from the lessons and the teachings in each season. We have to be present and a student during all of life's set backs and disappointments in order to appreciate the blessings we have and to prepare for the tests that are still ahead of us.

Sometimes things are taken away from us and we are stripped of our possessions to see if we are able to know that the only thing we need to sustain us is our prayers and our faith in the Creator. Even though we feel as if we are alone and our world has been turned upside down, are we able to be still and know the Creator is with us? My father always taught me to be still and calm and not get caught up in all the energy of adverse circumstances. There is incredible truth in that spiritual teaching. Another way to say that is: "Stay in balance and centered on your path, no matter what challenges you encounter that try to pull you off course."

Hurricanes are a perfect example of the truth in this teaching. Hurricanes are powerful and violent storms of nature that include rain, tornados, hail and winds that reach hundreds of miles per hour. Their destructive force is unimaginable and those who have witnessed their sheer magnitude and force can attest to it. However, in the center of any hurricane it is peaceful and calm, the skies are blue and the sun shines bright. It is the "Eye" of the storm. But if you step out of the eye of the storm in any direction you will immediately be thrust into a frenzy of energy and chaos that will consume you and take you where IT wants to take you.

It is the same in life. When we stay in the eye or the center of life's hurricanes, we do not allow the circumstances or seasons of life to control us and spin us into a frenzy of chaos. It is only when we move away from our path that we run the risk of getting thrown into the upheaval that is always whirling around us in life. The Creator wants us to stay centered with our focus upon Him so that we are not distracted and become off course. Our prayers are the tools with which we accomplish this. Through *The Medicine of Prayer* we are able to make sure the compass of our purpose reads straight and true so that we are always navigating life accurately. Focusing on our prayers and exercising our faith ensures that we will always respond well to the challenges we face in life and gives us the ability to keep things in context.

But, when we get caught up in other people or the circumstances of the day, we find ourselves reacting not responding to the seasons of our lives. Because of the challenges I have faced in life, I now understand better what my father meant by teaching me to respond and not react. It is only through *The Medicine of Prayer* that we are able to find the cure for our frustrations, anxiety and fear. We begin to understand that we are never alone nor without the Creator.

Through *The Medicine of Prayer* we come to know compassion, resilience and peace in times of change. We become people of compassion and resilience because of the compassion we experience from the Creator each time we are resilient and have faith our prayers will be answered. Thus peace is brought into our life and we see the beauty of living in the eye of all life's storms.

When you are blessed to be the recipient of compassion in your time of need, you can't help but give that compassion back to others when you see them in need.

Even if that moment comes several years later in a restaurant like the one you worked at in a much earlier season of your life.

Chapter Five

- The Long Walk -

"Love your family. Tell them you love them. Hold your family and hug them. Life is short. Don't make it full of regret too. Prayers to you!"

Throughout these difficult times when everything in my life was shifting like quicksand, there was one constant, stabilizing factor – my grandparents. Now that we were living with them, there was day-to-day contact with their love, wisdom and guidance. The bond was strong. My day began and ended with the words of my grandparents and the warmth of their presence. Having them near during this time was invaluable and it brought a great amount of stability to my life. And, as always, I helped Pop in his garden when I wasn't in Tulsa at work.

My grandparents' house was medium size with three bedrooms, one and a half baths and a joined living room/dining room. The kitchen was pretty small but my grandmother, Wilma Helen Davis or Nan as we called her, made culinary magic in that room. The meals she cooked and the taste of her cooking have yet to be outdone in any meals I have ever had since.

Her menu was based in southern comfort food and is now synonymous with memories of that time of my life. Each meal she prepared took me away from the struggles life had brought to my family. The aroma of her chicken fried steak and mashed potatoes and one of her incredible home made pies cooking in the oven would cause my shoulders to relax, ease my tension, calm my worries and serve as the best security blanket anyone could have wrapped me in at the time.

Needless to say, I savored those smells and ate each of those meals as if I already knew how priceless they would be to me later in life. And of course there was always an abundance of Pepsi in glass bottles in the refrigerator. That whole time seemed like I was living my own real life Norman Rockwell painting. Watching my Nan with her hair pinned back in a bun, sweating as she labored over the stove and cooked -- doing her part to contribute to the whole of our family.

Outside their house was a medium sized front yard, a laundry room and storage that were attached to the house along with a covered patio. Then there was the backyard that contained the garden and included various fruit trees: pear, apple and even a peach tree.

The back yard spanned from one side of the property to the other. On one end was a growth of blackberries and raspberries. Next to that there was a watermelon, strawberry and cantaloupe patch. We even grew pumpkins there. Next to that area was the garden proper with every vegetable you can imagine. We had rows of corn, potatoes, onions, radishes, rhubarb, carrots and even tomato vines to name a few.

Every year when I helped my grandfather harvest the food from his garden, my grandmother would begin "canning" a large portion of each vegetable and fruit to "put up" that food. Until next year's garden was harvested, this would be our canned food which supplied the majority of everything we ate and enjoyed at dinner. The process of canning food was an intense amount of work and an art in itself that I regretfully never paid enough attention to remember how to do. Nan was a master at it though, and after a few days of canning, their storage area outside looked like a section of a small grocery store. There was a great sense of pride that I felt from both of my grandparents after all the work had been done and the food was put up.

Today we take so much for granted with our food and the manner in which it grows and arrives at our dinner table -- a luxury that my grandparents were not familiar with. They were involved in each step of the process from beginning to end. I watched my grandfather spend hours looking at which were the best seeds to use for planting that year's garden. It was important to get it right from the first step in the process. Though most kids would have probably been bored to tears, I loved the minutes and hours that comprised those days in my life. I probably picked out and brought to him every package of seeds in the store to ask if he liked them and if they would be good for the garden.

Our extended stay with my grandparent's was okay with me but my father had been on his own and providing for himself and his own family for many years. Living again with his mother and father was a daily reminder of a situation he had no desire to be in. I believe my father was teetering in and out of depression during this time. He was very angry and I cannot imagine to this day the feelings he internalized. He wasn't mean to us or to my grandparents, but it didn't take a whole lot for other people to become the object of his pent up anger. Having worked so hard for so many years to achieve success in his businesses, then to lose it all at the hands of a family member, let alone his own brother, must have been daily mental torture for Dad. But he was a survivor, a good father and an incredible salesman and always did what he could to provide for us.

When the school year began that fall, it would be time for my junior year in high school. My mother decided I should stop working and return to my studies. A new school had opened and she wanted me to go there – Metro Christian Academy. Everyone in Tulsa referred to it as simply, "Metro." It was a private school and where the money was to come from for tuition I didn't know. But like I said, Mom always believed that where there was a will, there was a way.

I wanted to go back to school too and be around kids my age and have a social life. Some of my friends went to this new school and what piqued my interest even more was they had a good football team. It sounded like a lot of fun and the return to an age appropriate life that I had tuned out in order to focus on my responsibilities to my family.

Again, I didn't know how it was all going to come together. But I had the will, so surely there must be a way. Most of the other kids' parents were doctors or lawyers, while my Dad was making a living however he could and my Mom was cleaning houses. I would have to make a go of it on my own and not be afraid to stand alone in a new school. But that was exactly what Dad and Mom always told me to never be afraid to do. Good thing, because I definitely wasn't going to make new friends or be accepted at Metro because my parents were golf buddies with other kids' parents or had any high society affiliation within the Tulsa community at large.

So, I was constantly worrying and concerned as to how all this was going to work out and come to pass. Despite my worry, I tried to hold on to the faith that there would be a way. I kept up with my summer job, because we would definitely need the money and continued to push forward. My Mom knew some of the people running the school and met with them and explained our situation.

She worked out a plan with the school for me to start my junior year in September 1985.

Part of that plan was a partial "scholarship" awarded to families with income challenges. It would require me to do community service each weekend at an elder's house. After school I was to go over to the elder's home and whatever she had for me to do, I would do it; laying stones, cleaning out a spare room, mowing her yard. For this she would pay part of my tuition. This scholarship was more like a tuition loan that was paid back through my community service. Additionally, in order for me to start school as a junior, I was going to have to take some night classes to get enough credits to complete my sophomore year.

I learned a valuable lesson for my life from this experience: you do appreciate things you have to work for way more than the things that don't require you to make any sacrifice nor pay any price. With the arrangements my Mom made, things were looking up, but it was going to take some hard work and focus on my part to get there. So, when most kids were enjoying the last part of their summer, I enrolled in night school and got my credits in order to begin the fall semester as a junior in high school. Life was moving forward.

Prior to the beginning of school, there was a picnic being held for all new students at a park in Tulsa. It was a chance to see old friends and meet new students and my teachers. I was so excited to attend this event and begin to get back to school.

Before leaving my grandparents' house in Claremore to attend the picnic, I didn't get a chance to have my usual goodbye with Nan. She had recently taken a fall and broken her hip. Nan's health had never been good. She was always dealing with poor circulation and respiratory problems. After her fall she had hip surgery and was asleep recovering and getting some much needed rest. Before leaving I went into her bedroom and there I saw her sleeping peacefully. I went to wake her and say goodbye but then stopped myself, deciding to let her be and not disturb her. So I left and headed to Tulsa.

For the first time in a long time, I spent the day being a teenager at the picnic. It was a rare day for me to just have fun. I couldn't help smiling on the drive home to Claremore that night. I sped along with the windows down, reliving the evening with the radio blasting in the background. It felt like things were finally heading in the right direction in my life.

When I got home that night, I found my sister, Angelique, sitting in the front room in darkness. The house was unusually still, except that I could tell Angelique was crying. I called for my grandmother. I called again and then ran into her room. She wasn't there. Neither was my grandfather nor my dad. Everything was wrong and I feared the worst. I still have no clear memory of what happened next.

My sister will tell you that she had never heard me scream before that night. She will tell you that I went to my grandmother's room and grabbed up her blanket, still calling her name through my tears. And she will tell you that she was unable to stop me, to hold or comfort me before I careened out of the house into the night, out of reach. Nan was gone. I ran and ran and ran.

What I do remember is standing alone in the night, in the middle of the street looking up at the sky and talking to her, saying what I would have wanted to say had I been given the chance to say good bye. In those moments, I was basically making my peace with her. I knew her health was growing weak but I never anticipated that she would be taken from us so soon. That night I learned that death does not make appointments and we never know the day or the hour in which our time on this Earth will expire. Life became more precious to me that night.

The sky was really clear and very bright the night of my grandmother's death. Looking up I recognized Orion's Belt. Those three stars all in order in the sky were very significant to me in that moment. Nothing shone as bright in the sky as they did and I looked at them and I thought of my grandmother, my grandfather and I. It's as if there was a star for each of us. We had been like three peas in a pod and now one of us was no longer on Earth. I never paid much attention to Orion's Belt before that night, but every time I have witnessed it since, I am reminded of the lifelong bond I have with my grandparents. I remember praying for strength. Praying for my grandfather. And praying for the Creator to just help us.

My Nan was gone and at a time when I wanted to show her I was going to make it; I was going to go back to school, play sports and do good with my life. I needed her there for me, for us and for my grandfather. I wanted her to see me become somebody and to be proud of me. But just like that, my security blanket was taken away and I felt vulnerable to the world. My friend was gone. It devastated me.

Later, when I finally returned to the house, a song was playing on the radio that spoke to what I was feeling that night. It was James Taylor's "Fire and Rain." When I'd left the house that afternoon the thought never crossed my mind that I'd never see my grandmother again; that I wouldn't be able to share the highlights of the school picnic with her. I couldn't get that one particular lyric out of my mind, "…I always thought that I'd see you again."

After my numbness and grief began to wear off, I became more concerned about my sister, my father and mostly my grandfather. My grandparents had been nearly inseparable and it was hard to picture them without each other. My grandfather had stood by Nan's side through all her medical problems and had taken care of her and pampered her better than any caregiver could have done. When she couldn't get out of bed he would sit and rub her forehead or brush her hair with such gentleness and care that I am sure it was healing to her. In his actions, my grandfather showed me the meaning of love and how deep love can be. I had intense concern for Pop and drew closer to him than ever during this time.

The death of Nan had also brought me front and center with the understanding that we are not promised tomorrow. None of us are. So, I clung to my grandfather and absorbed each day and moment I had with him. Nan's funeral was really the first funeral I had ever attended and I remember my Pop being so strong. We celebrated Nan's life that day and yet laying her to rest may have been one of the saddest days of my grandfather's life -- saying goodbye to his soul mate. They say that people can die from a broken heart. Well, Pop buried half of his with Nan that day.

One night, soon after Nan's funeral, Pop and I went to eat at a small local Mexican restaurant in Claremore called Taco Tico. As we were eating, I asked him if he thought that people could come back after they had died and talk to people or at least let them know they were still there. I told him if something ever happened to me, I loved him so much that, if it were possible, I would do everything I could to come back and let him know I was all right. He told me he didn't know if that was possible, but he felt Nan's presence with him a lot of the time. In fact, the night after she passed, he had a dream of her calming him and letting him know she was okay.

I asked him if anything ever happened to him, would he please try to come back and let me know he was okay? Pop told me to not worry. He was sure that if he could... he would. I was asking him because my world had been so shaken from my grandmother's passing. The loss of her in my life caused me to cling tighter to my grandfather. I sure didn't want to lose my Pop too. I just wanted to hear some assurance from him that he would be with me always. I really didn't know if what I was asking for was realistic but I needed to believe it was.

My father was of special concern to me during these days because of how close he was to Nan, and I feared that this would be the proverbial straw that broke the camel's back. It was too much for him to stay in the house where his mother had lived. Everything there was a reminder of her. Every dish of hers that we tried to cook just resulted in us talking about her and feeling a deep sadness that she was no longer with us.

Dad could no longer deal with the additional stress that living in his parents' house was causing him and us. He went to Tulsa one day and found a house that we could afford and asked for us to come with him. Dad wanted Pop to come and live in our new home too. But that was not an option for Pop. He had made up his mind to stay in their home. I begged him to come with us, but he wasn't budging. In his gentle way he told me: "Go on, I will be okay and don't you worry about me. I'll be right as rain." But I was torn about leaving Pop alone in an empty house.

We weren't able to move into the new house until after school started, so at first I made the forty-minute drive from Claremore to Tulsa each morning. I was able to escape into football. It was a way for me to get a lot of my own pent up anger and aggression out. I even started going out with the co-captain of the cheerleading squad. It kind of made me feel like I was having somewhat of a normal life.

My girlfriend's family was like the poster family for the American Dream -- everything my family wasn't at the time. Her mother was very involved with the cheerleading squad and also the school's secretary, while her dad was in charge of the school's concessions and helped out with the athletic program. She was the girl everyone knew. They had a dog out back, a station wagon, a Jacuzzi, a family room. It was a totally different dynamic than the life I was living and I basked in the warmth of it each chance I got. Knowing them was a blessing for me.

I was internalizing much of what I was going through during this time. It had become my default reaction to strife. I had taken standing alone to a whole other level and I didn't go out of my way to be very social. Not that I was rude or unfriendly – but there was a whirlwind of energy going on beneath the surface of my existence and I was doing my best to keep moving forward and not let the pain and hurt of my experiences slow me down.

Not many of my friends had the same lunch hour as I did and so I would go sit in the football locker room and eat my food alone. Life seemed way more complicated for me than the lives of my classmates. I often felt like I didn't have much in common with them and the truth of the matter was, I didn't. One day while I was eating my lunch in front of my locker a kid named Paul came in with his lunch. He played football too, was new to the school and I guess he had the same lunch idea as me. We began to talk and the more we talked the more I found out how much we had in common. One thing he mentioned was, his mom was a maid like my mom. From that moment, we hit it off and became best friends.

These were turbulent but formative days in my life. I recount them with an appreciation of the Creator and all the many times that the Creator sheltered and shielded me. Each day that I lived I was learning to become a man and simultaneously growing in my spiritual walk. I may not have been able to identify it as that at the time, but going to Metro gave me something that a public school would not have allowed.

At Metro the teachers and the staff could openly speak about the Creator, prayer and faith. I have to say it helped me greatly! Again, whether I accounted for it at the time or not there was Bible class everyday and chapel on Wednesday. Aside from the positive outlets that football and studies afforded me, being able to feed my spirit was vital to me. My walk with the Creator began to be more and more intimate. The way my family life was going, and trying to keep up at school, this was a time when I could have easily lost track of my connection with the Creator. There was all the normal teenage experimentation going on in high school for me to get distracted with, let alone all the things happening at home.

Today, I can acknowledge the blessing it was to spend time in chapel every week to renew my relationship with the Creator and help me to maintain focus on my studies and sports. Even though I found myself occasionally falling asleep in class, mostly due to the two-hour round trip commute from Claremore to school, week by week my spirit was being healed and made stronger. I was physically able to rise to the occasion. I was beginning to understand the power of *The Medicine of Prayer*.

I began making new friends and I beat out a two-year starter on the football team to be named the 1st string wide receiver. I was moving forward and doing well. I would often think of my Nan during class or on my drives to and from school, wishing that she could see how well I was doing. I knew she would be proud of me. Missing her made me appreciate even more looking up into the stands on Friday nights to see my grandfather's face. Nan was there and represented by his presence.

Through my prayers and continuing to push forward I was growing up fast. I had dealt with so many real life matters in such a short time in my young life, that it made me appreciate my journey in a larger way than I felt any of my classmates understood. I would walk down the halls and realize how trivial some of their concerns were compared to some of what life had already shown me. I could appreciate the sacrifice my mom was making for me and the houses she had to clean each day in order for me to be able to attend class at Metro. I was also able to come to terms with the inevitable long walk that each of us, and those whom we love, must take.

The grief of my grandmother's passing took its deepest toll on my grandfather. After her death, he grew progressively weaker. In late Fall of that year, my father, my sister and I moved back to Tulsa. As he said he would, Pop stayed in Claremore in the home he had shared with Nan. I was getting busier with football, schoolwork and managing my home life. Even though we had gotten back a bit of our family's independence by returning to Tulsa and into our own home, that didn't mean we were out of the woods yet.

Dad still did not have steady income. To get some cash flow going again he began selling all the possessions that we no longer needed or had use for by holding garage sales at our new house. When he ran out of our items to sell he began going to other garage sales, flea markets and antique stores to buy items he knew he could sell at our garage sale to a growing list of clients he had. Within a short window of time and evoking his entrepreneurial spirit, he turned this weekend garage sale concept into a seven day a week business that put food on our table.

But there were also times when he didn't make enough to pay the light or water bills. So, I would get up extra early before school and go to a health club we'd received a free membership to and shower and get ready for school. I didn't get frustrated and even decided that this was a perfect opportunity to get a workout in before school. By the time the 8:00 A.M. bell rang for my first class of the day, I had already been up for three hours getting prepared for school.

All in all it made me thankful for when we did get a bit of money and everything was paid up. But if things got tough again, I knew it wasn't the end of the world. I was becoming a survivor and more determined to continue moving forward each day.

After football season ended I had a surplus of time on my hands after school. When I had been working the previous year, it felt good to be able to make money and I loved the independence that came with that. Times were still tough and I knew my dad was doing his best to provide for us. I didn't want to add to that by asking for date money or money to buy things that I had my eye on at the mall. So I got a job at a local pizza shop to supplement our income and give me some spending money.

That winter our family situation changed again when I got called out of class and was told that my grandfather had been admitted to the hospital. Pop never complained and he seemingly was never sick, at least not for very long. So when I heard he voluntarily went to the hospital, I knew something must be wrong.

Immediately, I drove to Claremore Indian Hospital to see him. When I got there he was sitting up in his hospital bed and in good spirits. He told me not to worry. He was going to be okay, if not, "Well," he said, "I have lived a long good life and I have no regrets." It made my heart sink to hear him say that. But I knew he was alone in this world without Nan and more than anything he longed for her. A few days later he was released from the hospital but he had been diagnosed with lung cancer.

For years Pop had been a cigarette smoker and as soon as I was old enough to know that cigarettes caused cancer, I would break his cigarettes any chance I got. Nan smoked too and her cigarettes were on my radar as well. My guerilla style attacks against their tobacco surplus would make them both pretty angry with me, but they knew why I was doing it. I simply didn't want anything to happen to them, especially not if it was by their own doing. It took no doctor to know that my grandmother's poor circulation was a direct result of her years of smoking and starving her body of much needed oxygen.

My grandfather began chemotherapy that January and by February he was in the hospital again. The chemotherapy had whittled away at him until he was a frail representation of the man I knew all my life. Then one day Pop took a turn for the worse. He was placed on life support and we all gathered at the hospital. It was very hard for me to see him with the little amount of life that was now left in his body.

My grandfather was a strong man who would have fought tooth and nail to beat cancer had my grandmother still been alive. But his loneliness had beat out his will to survive and I believe all he wanted was to be with her once again.

That evening, not long after reading him a poem I had written about all he meant to me, Pop let go of this life. I know he was overjoyed to see my Nan once again. I knew he was no longer suffering from the pain of his cancer and that his heart no longer had to yearn for my grandmother. But, I was overwhelmed with sorrow at his passing. I had lost not just my grandfather -- I lost my best friend.

We left the hospital and went to Pop's house to spend the night as it was very late and we were exhausted. I was sitting on the couch as everyone began to go to sleep, but I didn't want to move. So I sat alone in the dark thinking of him and the life we shared together. I breathed in all the things that smelled of him and spoke to his existence. I talked to him in the dark and let him know how much I loved him and needed him.

As I sat there alone that night I fell asleep on the couch thinking of how much I owed him for all he taught me. As I began to dream, I found myself standing at the edge of Pop's garden and just staring into it. It was beautiful. All the vegetables and fruits were ripe and ready to be picked. It was so green and bountiful. I could see the stalks of corn beginning to move and the movement was coming toward where I was standing. Then I could see Pop. He was walking toward me through the corn. My heart swelled and I was elated. He had come to see me in the same garden we had spent hours together till dark on so many evenings, with him imparting information to me in one way or another.

As I was standing there looking at him he came to the edge of the garden and talked to me. I told him how much I loved him and wanted to be with him. He told me everything would be okay and not to worry. He wanted me to try and help bring my uncle and my dad together -- to make peace. He asked if I could help him do that. I remember trying to reach for him to hug him but I couldn't move. I told him I would do my best to try to help dad and my uncle resolve their differences. He looked at me and said, "That's my boy." And then he turned to go. I didn't want him to leave. "Don't leave me," I said. But he told me he had to go and I would be okay. As he turned and walked into the garden I tried again to grab for his hand, but I still could not move.

And as he disappeared back into the row of lush green and yellow corn, the garden began to dissolve behind him. Then it was gone and I awoke. Pop had come back to me and he let me know he was okay like he said he would.

The next days and weeks were difficult to say the least. I remember attending Pop's funeral and seeing the multitude of people who came to pay their last respects. There was no doubt that Pop touched the lives of all those he came in contact with and on that day they, in return, came to appreciate his life. Right up to the day he went to the hospital complaining of shortness of breath and a pain in his side, he had been working construction. On one of the last jobs Pop worked, he made such an impact on one of his co-workers that on the day of his funeral that man came and wept uncontrollably at the loss of my grandfather. He just kept repeating over and over again what a good man Pop was and how compassionate he was.

Shortly after Pop's death it became clear that there was to be more upheaval. While Pop lay dying, my uncle talked him into making him the executor of his will, removing my father from that capacity. This authority gave my uncle final say in all matters regarding the estate of my grandfather, enraging my father further. It wasn't that there was any money to be had from the estate, it was the principle of the matter. The disdain between my father and uncle became irreversibly wedged. This was not a good start to the promise I'd made my grandfather to bring peace between his sons.

The sense of loss I felt after my grandfather's death was as if someone had removed my arm and leg and I was now half of who I had been when Pop was alive. I have never met another man like him and though there are many good men who have walked this Earth, none of them were my Pop and none of them had a garden like his.

The storms that raged inside me after the death of my grandfather were torrential. However, when I was able to focus on the Creator and not the roar of my problems, the screams of distractions became whispers and then ultimately they were silenced. When you have witnessed those roars silenced by the

Creator they are far less likely to intimidate you and pull you away from your path the next time you hear them.

The Medicine of Prayer taught me that if there is one lifeline that is of the utmost importance during the raging storms we encounter on our path, it is the lifeline of prayer. Our prayers are what allow us to stay in constant connection with the Creator for guidance and direction to navigate the currents and tides of our struggle.

Through my Pop's death and burial I began to understand the impact our lives can have on those around us. The man who grieved so strongly at Pop's funeral may have never told him all the things he expressed to me and my family that day, yet the impact my grandfather had on him was obvious and beyond words. I understood that if we do our best in life and look to the Creator to forge ahead and find our path, we cannot help but positively impact other people.

The Medicine of Prayer is so strong that when we are walking in faith and on the path we were born to walk and come into contact with others, they can get a dose of that powerful medicine too. When we are utilizing the power that comes from *The Medicine of Prayer*, we may never know all of the people that we empower and may never be able to measure just how much good we were able to do with each day of our life. We should all have that "problem" as it would cause the world to be a much better place for us all.

I also understood the connection that we are able to have here on Earth between this world and the next. The dream I had of my grandfather coming to me was so powerful and so real that I count it as my first vision. I had asked Pop if he were able, to come and let me know he was okay. And he did. But as a young man, I actually didn't think that it would be possible for him to do this.

When Pop came to me in my dream I believe the Creator knew I needed that closure in order to move on with my life.

Selu or Corn is very significant to our Cherokee people. One thing that Corn means to us is Life. That my grandfather came to me in the garden through the rows of corn symbolized to me that he was coming to me "re-born." I wasn't able to move and couldn't touch him in my dream because he was purified through this re-birth and was now with the Creator. I wasn't able to understand it to that degree when I woke up from the dream that night, but I did feel a peace come over me and I was able to fall back asleep. I began letting go of Pop in that moment.

The next time I looked up into the night sky after that and saw the three stars of Orion's Belt, I knew Pop was now there shinning bright with my Nan and that one day when my journey on Earth was complete - I would join them. Many years later while visiting the Passamaquoddy Indian reservation in Maine, a woman came to me and told me she had a dream of me before I arrived. She had looked into the sky in her dream and saw thousands of stars moving in one direction in the sky and that when she looked back down all the stars were mirrored on the Earth by Native people. They were all walking together in the same direction and looking up and following one star in the sky and she said that star was me. That day she gave me the Passamaquoddy name Possasum or Star.

The symbolism of the star drew me back to my grandparents, Orion's Belt and the promise Pop had made to me -- always to be there with me and that everything was going to be alright.

Pop never broke promises.

☙

Chapter Six

– Purpose –

*"Success has no set formula. Realize you were born with a road map to success. Follow your map, not someone else's.
Their map will get you lost."*

With the deaths of my grandparents in such a short space of time, I learned to cherish each and every day with those whom I love. Through the love they shared together, I began to understand that life is too short to spend it arguing over petty differences and misunderstandings, like my father and uncle did. It was important to me to make the most of each day the Creator has given and use my time wisely. I was filled with grief and a heavy heart upon the passing of Pop and Nan. But, when I began to go to the Creator with my sorrow, that sorrow was lifted. I was able to focus on what my grandparents would have wanted for me and I put my energy into making them proud of me and fulfilling my destiny, instead of letting the grief turn to anger or some other negative emotion which only would have led me away from all the good in life.

It wasn't easy returning to school and focus on my studies after Pop's burial, yet I knew he would not want me to do anything but be my very best in life. And so I continued to push forward.

During this season of my life I realized that the Creator never gives us more than we can deal with, even though we may feel like the burden is overwhelming. Dealing with so much adversity in my early teens was shaping and defining my character and creating the strength and resilience I would need to draw from in order to reach my goals later in life. Once each of the storms of my life subsided and I was able to gather myself for a moment to reflect, I realized that I had weathered some very intimidating times. I may have been blown around a good bit, but for the most part, I was able to stay in the eye of those storms and remain calm, like my father taught me. Because I didn't get completely caught up in the moment, I was able to survive the tide.

However, going back to school after the death of my grandfather felt so trivial. When I would hear other kids complain about school, breaking up with their girlfriend or what new clothes they had to have, my mind would say, man you don't even know. My classmates just didn't have a clue about what difficulties were out there in life. Still, I was trying to fit in the best I could and going to school was like getting away from it all. It was a break from the seemingly constant barrage of trials and tribulations that I had been going through and it made getting decent grades and getting to class on time seem like a cakewalk. I was still working at the pizza shop and making my own money. I used that money to buy lunch at school, clothes and I would help out my family too.

We were far from living a worry free financial existence. Things were still tough. Often it was a struggle just to keep the lights and water on. When we couldn't find the money to pay the bills and the utilities did get turned off, we would use candles for light and for water we'd make a trip down to the gas station to fill up a large five-gallon water bottle from the station's water spigot. I made up my mind that what we had or what we didn't have wasn't going to determine my state of mind nor my future. I was thankful I had my family to lean on during this time.

It was sad for me to think though that the circumstances of the last several months had driven my mother and father apart. They were fighting hard to move forward individually, but I couldn't help think they could create so much more progress by coming together. I would have loved for them to reconcile and provide my sister and I with the sense of security that comes from a unified home. That wasn't to be.

In hindsight, I realize that these difficult times were developing within me character traits that I would need later in life. I didn't realize it then but my experiences were building strength within me that was based upon faith in the Creator. My faith and these character traits would give me the resolve to walk my path. Each day and each step prepared me more for the journey ahead. I was learning to keep moving forward and not sink into the quicksand of despair that seemed to always be treacherously close.

Mom and Dad didn't hang their head when things fell apart and they never gave up. They kept moving no matter how devastating the blows that life dealt them were. I realized we can't choose what comes our way but we can choose how we deal with it. Today in my talks I tell people: "Change your attitude and you will change your life!" I chose to view the situations I was going through optimistically, rather than pessimistically. If things went the wrong way and took me in a direction that I hadn't anticipated, I simply looked for the good in the new direction and began planning how to make the best of it. I count myself blessed that I was able, at a young age, to stay calm and know the Creator always had things under control. I attribute this ability directly to teachings from my mother and father.

At school I was doing my best to not be idle and stagnant. If I hadn't stayed busy I may very well have allowed my thoughts and worries to work overtime and create a world of fear and negativity.

My father's words would ring in my head: "Don't panic! The answers are usually right in front of you."

There is a story of a swimmer who went for a swim one day in the ocean. Not long into his swim he was caught in a riptide. As the tide began to push the swimmer out into the sea, he began to panic and began swimming furiously toward the shore. However, the tide just pulled him further away from the land. Near exhaustion and close to drowning, the swimmer decided to calm himself and rest by floating on his back with the tide. So the swimmer floated in the ocean and rested to regain his strength for another go at the shore. Several minutes later the swimmer rose up from his floating position and prepared for what he felt was going to be an even further swim to land. But to his amazement, as he looked around and gathered himself, the land was now actually closer than before. As he stayed calm and floated along, he realized the tide was actually now bringing him back toward the land. He got closer and closer and now was within a few hundred feet of the beach. He began swimming out of the pull of the weakened tide and not long after he walked ashore.

As he began his walk back up the beach to where he entered the water, he realized how close he had come to drowning. It was only when he let go and went with the tide that it allowed him to break free of it. Sure, he was now a few miles from where he wanted to be, but he didn't lose his life and he was back on solid ground. Most importantly, he learned a life saving lesson that would help him anytime he was ever in the ocean again. It's also a life lesson that we can all draw from.

In life we have to go through struggles to learn key lessons vital to our journey. There are often no other ways to gather the knowledge, wisdom and teachings that we need. We have to learn to let go and remain calm so that we can grow as a person. If we do, we are able to gather the lessons from each challenge enabling us to better prepare for the obstacles that lie ahead of us. We can choose to fight against things or we can realize that our challenges are vital to our progress -- life's difficulties are our teachers. They mold us and shape us and bring us greater understandings. The Creator provides us with these teachers, in order to broaden our view of our journey and enhance our ability to serve and protect it.

In any classroom the best environment for learning is a quiet and focused one. The same holds true when we are learning from our journey. We have to try to tune out the chaos and noise that come with our struggles and stay calm in the eye of the storm. Our struggle then takes place in a calm environment wherein we can focus on the lessons we are meant to learn. Of course it is not always easy to step aside during our difficulties and be "calm."

When challenges are coming at us from every direction we want to run, fight or stress out. But, we have to remember that through our faith and prayers to the Creator, we are able to rise above the greatest of challenges. Is there any challenge or obstacle that we know of in this life that is bigger than the Creator? Our abilities do begin and end, but the Creator's power is not measurable. We have to hit the "Creator Button" when it gets too much for us. I have hit that button more times than I can remember in my life. The Creator brings us the calm that we need during our trials and heals us through our prayers. This to me may be the clearest and most concise definition of *The Medicine of Prayer*.

If we allow our physical self to be consumed with everything that is trying to distract us, we may miss the teaching we are meant to receive. But, if we keep our eyes on the Creator and stay in constant communication through our prayers we are able to hear clearly and see all that we are being shown. We are also rejuvenated and strengthened in order to carry on and get beyond our struggles. Our faith and belief is increased immeasurably and we understand the magnificence of the Creator more. He does have it all under control!

During difficult times it's so easy to begin to feel alone and as if we were the only person who has ever experienced a trial like the one we are facing. It is easy to begin to think that you have been left deserted in your struggle. We might think that there is nothing or no one there for us. But if we turn to *The Medicine of Prayer* we are able to stay the course in the darkest of nights, never becoming lost in the ocean of our trials. Our prayers become like our homing beacon, signaling to the Creator that we have trust and faith that He has a higher purpose and calling for our lives. By exercising our faith and remaining calm we allow the Creator to lead and guide us through life's tribulations.

When we show the Creator our faith and that we believe in His power and abilities, we allow ourselves to become the recipients of His power and ability manifested through our lives. Just like that swimmer, it doesn't mean that things don't get scary when we leave the safety of the shore and begin to feel the riptide of our challenges. But if we stay calm and keep our trust in the Creator, we will always be able to take action accordingly and end up right where we are supposed to be. When we are back on land we will realize the Creator knew the outcome all along and we were always safely in the grasp of the Creator's plan for our lives.

Many times during Wednesday chapel at Metro I felt like the message given by the speaker that day was aimed directly at me. The words spoken there lifted my spirit and adjusted my view of all that was going on in my life. I was realizing my challenges do not in themselves determine their outcome, but rather I determine how I deal with my challenge and therefore I can have an impact on the outcome.

I thought of how just a few months before, I was bussing tables and wondering how I was ever going to get back in school. My current reality of being back in school seemed so far away then. I thought of all the work and effort that I had put forth to keep pushing forward to get where I was. I thought of the devastating loss of my grandmother and grandfather and how hard it was to lose them both so close together. As I was thinking about these things, I thanked the Creator for the strength to carry on and how blessed I was to have made so much progress despite so many challenges.

Maybe to others it didn't seem as if I had progressed much. I may not have been ranked very high above zero if the world was to have judged me based on its standards and measurements for success. But I was doing my very best everyday to forge ahead and I know the Creator knew the condition of my heart. I kept moving forward, taking one day at a time.

My girlfriend and I were still an item and Paul and I had become even better friends. I look back now and realize that the Creator placed both of them in my life to help me and fill me up with laughter and companionship. They were both answers to prayer and gifts from the Creator, even if I didn't understand that then. Being able to hang out with them and get away from the pressures of my life and those that come along with high school revitalized me. I didn't pay too much attention to peer pressure and the trivial designations by the "in crowd" of what was and wasn't cool on any given day. Metro required everyone to wear a uniform, so I was lucky that I didn't need a full wardrobe consisting of the latest fashion trends for school to be considered "in." You could wear blue khakis or grey dress pants with a white or blue polo or dress shirt. I remember I had one pair of blue khakis my junior year of high school. I ironed those blue pants so much by the end of the year the crease was like a white line down the front of each leg. I guess I had enough swagger at seventeen years of age that I pulled it off and I wore those khakis with pride. Because I had confidence and wore them like they were "hot" nobody said anything about it. In reality they were all that I had and no one was going to make me feel like I was less than. I had already learned from my job bussing tables that my occupation did not define who I was and the condition of my uniform was not going to define what kind of student I was either.

As the school year wound to a close, Mom was still cleaning houses and I was still working each weekend doing community service to pay for my tuition. In order for Mom to pay my tuition something had to give. She didn't have enough money left each month to pay rent for an apartment, so she was still living with the same friend who'd been gracious enough to open up her home months ago. By the end of my junior year of high school I felt I had earned every second of that school year. I was overjoyed that I was one summer away from starting my final year of high school! Nothing had come easy and I was learning to fight to get ahead in life.

Each week in chapel I would pray for my family and for the strength to stay focused and to not give up myself. I prayed for the ability to maintain balance and not to get caught up in the circumstances, to respond to challenges and not react to them. I was learning that through *The Medicine of Prayer* we are given access to a wealth of strength via our communication and connectedness to the Creator. But I was also learning that what *The Medicine of Prayer* won't do, is walk your path for you. Even the Bible says: "Faith without works is dead." My sister and I were still staying with my father and it was touch and go with finances and keeping a positive attitude. But I kept moving forward and I was sure Pop and Nan would have been proud of me.

At the beginning of the summer some tension had arisen between my father and I. So, I chose to go and stay with mom. Mom was now sharing a two-bedroom apartment with a woman who was a friend of one of her clients. Mom slept on the couch and I slept in the spare room on the floor on a pallet. I decided I was going to try and make as much money as I could that summer and set out to help her get an apartment and save up some money for tuition too.

That summer I got a job at Taco Bueno, a local fast food restaurant. It kind of worked out nicely because I would eat there all the time and now I got an employee meal discount. But eating it everyday got old quick. I realized that one job wasn't going to get me where I wanted to be in achieving my goals. The lady my mom was staying with knew a friend who had his own small landscaping company. She called him and told him about me. It just so happened he was looking to hire someone to help him for the summer and I joined his landscaping crew. Each morning he'd pick me up and I'd ride in the back of this old truck with the lawnmowers and equipment. We rode all over Tulsa in the 100 and whatever degree temperatures, and he would drop me off when we were done with work. I would then go to work at the fast food restaurant in the evenings.

Not the most prestigious time in my life. But it was work. Now, when I see somebody doing a job like manual labor, I don't have anything but respect for them, because they are willing to make an honest living, instead of selling drugs or stealing. I tell people all the time, you may not be able to find a job in the work you want to do, but there is a job out there, your ego just isn't allowing you to do it. Again, my mom taught me, where there's a will there's a way. If you want it bad enough you will make it happen. And if it means taking care of my family – there's not a dish I wouldn't wash. I have seen people who go through a hard time and they do nothing to get themselves out of the situation except look for someone else to give them a handout to get back on their feet rather than pulling themselves up by their own bootstraps. There is always a way to rise up, but you have to be willing to do what it takes and make the best of it.

We always have at least one choice: to do something or not do something… to quit or to keep going and persevere. It may not be the most glamorous or prideful existence for the moment, but there are lessons in those moments that will last a lifetime. The Creator does not want us to wait around and expect someone else to carry our burdens. We have each been born with God given abilities and the Creator wants us to use those, in order to develop them and apply them in all ways. Those abilities enhance who we are in good times and sustain us in bad times. When we act upon our faith and continue to walk forward through difficult times utilizing our abilities, the Creator will open up the floodgates of blessings upon us.

I recall my father telling new employees who were eager to impress him in their new position at his company: "Don't tell me what you can do. Show me what you can do." That is in essence, exactly what the Creator says to us: "Don't tell me you appreciate the life and ability I have given you. You must show me by using your gifts to live the life you have been born to live and fulfill your destiny." When the Creator sees that by our actions we are walking our talk, we will be blessed in ways we may have not thought possible. Our actions and good works become like a key that unlocks and activates all the blessings and abundance along our path which the Creator already prepared and had waiting for us.

By the end of the summer I had moved back in with my Dad and my sister. Dad had also gotten a new job that required him to travel a lot. My parent's divorce had become final too. It was apparent to my sister and I that they would not be getting back together and that our family would never exist as it had in our childhood. It didn't take long for Dad to begin excelling at his job and in a short time we moved into a better house. I began my senior year of high school filled with conflicting emotions. I felt more and more like the kids at school were on some other wave length and I threw myself into playing football and hanging with Paul and my girlfriend in my spare time.

When Dad had to go out of town, which was quite a bit, I took care of my sister. I got myself up to go to school, cooked our food, washed our clothes and whatever else needed to be done. There was no one there to make sure I did anything. It would have been easy for me to have not done my homework or gone to school at all for that matter. But, I didn't want to let my family down and I knew they were still working their hardest to make things better for us all. Dad would drive hundreds of miles all night from where he was working, just to get back to see us. He would stock up our groceries and give us some money for whatever may come up that week and then he would have to leave again. But we knew he hated being away from us and he wanted nothing more than to be at home everyday. My father was giving us 110% and doing what he had to do to provide for my sister and me. I couldn't let him down, so there was no choice for me other than to be responsible and follow through with my end of the deal by graduating from high school.

Before the start of that year's football season I watched a college football game on TV where all the players were wearing a black piece of tape on the back of their helmets to signify a recent death in their program. When our practices began the next week, I put a small piece of black tape on the back of my helmet in memory of my grandparents. Pop had been up in the stands last year for all my games and it was tough to know this year he wouldn't be there. Each time I looked at that tape on my helmet before practice or a game I vowed to play as hard as I could as if Pop was watching me all the time. Because I believed he was.

While other kids were planning their college careers, I was just trying to make it through to the end of the year. Mom and Dad definitely did not have the money to pay for me to go to college. So I knew without them having to say anything, if I was going to continue my education I'd have to go on a football scholarship or get a job to pay my way through college.

There was excitement about graduation, but also an uncertainty about what would come next. I put a lot of time into becoming the best football player I could be. It was my passion and the perfect way for me to physically release all the tension that had been stored up inside me and not get in trouble for doing it. It was also potentially becoming my ticket to a college education. My high school head coach had his favorites on the team and I got my first dose of politics. I worked hard and played well through my senior season of football. But it was becoming evident that my coach wasn't pushing me to college scouts as much as he was some of the other players. I knew that if I was going to get a scholarship, I would have to make it happen for myself.

What I also remember about that time was taking senior pictures. Kids were talking about what their parents were planning for graduation, their pride in taking them to get their senior pictures, what they would wear. Time was running out for me to get my pictures taken by the deadline. Dad had been out of town and I didn't want to stress him out because I knew he already had all he could deal with on the road. We were supposed to wear a suit. I didn't have one. I remember going into his closet to find something that didn't look too big. I found a blazer, one of his ties and added them to my blue school pants and a shirt. I went there alone. When I look back at that picture it reminds me of how I just kept pushing forward.

After graduation, I continued working. There was the chance to go to Kansas on a football scholarship. I took the recruiting trip up there, but I didn't want to play there. I had decided that I wanted to study law and the University of Tulsa was known to have a really good law school. And, I wanted to play for Tulsa!

Angelique had started going out with the man who would become my brother-in-law. I really looked up to Steve and wanted to play ball where he did. He was a really good athlete and I knew he would make it to the pros. This was a path I could follow, too. I went to enroll there and was told how to apply for Pell Grants and student loans. Coming out of my experience at Metro, I knew I would have to work harder for the better education and to get what would benefit me in the long term. Even then, I knew I wouldn't be able to play football forever. But I could pay for my education through football. I went and met with the coach and told them what I wanted. He said he'd love to have me. My goal was to try out as a walk on and then get a scholarship if I worked hard and proved myself on the field.

Even though I was going to school in my hometown, it felt like I was really "going away" to school. At the end of the summer, my Mom was planning to move back to California. Dad was constantly on the road. Angelique had an apartment on the other side of town. My girlfriend left for college and we decided it was best to break up. I had no car, so the campus became my home. It was the first time I was really alone. Just like with going for my senior pictures, I was getting along on my own. No one was with me figuring out my class schedule or setting up my dorm room. My mom brought me and my stuff to the dorm and then she had to leave for California. I was kind of like that fish out of water. But there was so much going on I didn't have time to feel too lonely.

My research into pre-law showed that most lawyers had majored in either Political Science or English. I chose Political Science. Very soon I knew it wasn't going to work. As a Native person, I couldn't be silent when the professor started going on about how wonderful the Federalist Papers were, and trying to convince us that the authors were heroes. We had a few exchanges during class and I knew my time studying Political Science was going to be short. I stuck it out for the first quarter and then switched my major to Business.

However, I was having much more success with football. When I made the team, I felt like I was living a dream. Football became everything for me. I would play at Tulsa, and after college I would try out for a pro team. I had the skills and playing for the University of Tulsa gave me confidence that I was moving in the right direction, that I was on the way to fulfilling my purpose.

For homecoming that season we played the University of Oklahoma. After the game, I went to the athletic dorm to change. My plan was to meet up with a girl I had my eye on. When I came back down, there was my dad waiting for me. He had come back into town for the game. I decided to have dinner with my Dad and asked him to wait a minute till I found the girl to set up a date for later. Well, I couldn't find her, but when I returned I found my dad having a fight with seven guys. I didn't know what caused the fight, but regardless, I wouldn't let my Dad fight alone. By the time it was all over, I ended up with a broken hand. I was going to be out for the rest of the football season.

The cast came off in time for spring training. When I had first reported for football out of high school, I came in underweight and so I began lifting weights to bulk up. I came in at 190 and by spring training I had put on 45lbs of muscle. I was on an ultra mission! I would work out three times a day. I was sure to be in shape to continue my college football career. We had a coordinated off-season training schedule where we would workout in groups as a team.

During one of these sessions, I was doing squats with the weights. I felt something give in my back and I dropped the weights on to the safety rail of the squat rack. It wasn't too painful…no big deal, I thought, and kind of blew it off. But soon it got to the point where I couldn't run or do any conditioning. It was determined that I had suffered a stress fracture on one of the vertebrae in my back and I realized I wouldn't be able to follow that dream of having a successful college football career to pay for my education. Once again, another door was slamming shut in my face. Clearly, my purpose was not to be a pro football player. Although football was what I wanted, it didn't appear to be what I was born to pursue. Time once again to regroup.

That summer I shared an apartment in Tulsa with my sister. She was cheerleading for a semi-pro basketball team and working to perform as a singer. Angelique was all about performing arts and she could sing -- she had the talent and the personality of a performer. I never was like that, but I enjoyed music.

Ours was a musical household and I was a fan of rap music – Public Enemy, NWA, Rakim, Big Daddy Kane, Heavy D and lots of R&B. I remember on the drives from Claremore to Tulsa listening to Run DMC. Michael Jackson was always huge with me. Growing up, my parents listened to a lot of Motown, Vanilla Fudge, Tower of Power, Chicago, funk, soul music; Stevie Wonder was my parent's favorite singer, along with Diana Ross. The first concert my parents took me to was "Chicago" at the Hollywood Bowl in Los Angeles when I was only two years old. I love hearing live music -- hearing what people do when they feel something and turn it into music. It's kind of magical. I didn't think it was something I'd ever do publicly. I'd sit in my room listening to classical music and writing. It was like whatever the music told me I would write that story -- more like poems and stories. But it was just something I did in my down time to relax and get things off my chest.

My job that summer was at the exclusive Ralph Lauren store in Tulsa. I wanted to work in that elegant environment and I knew, when I went for the interview that I didn't have the wardrobe to work there. But I had the ambition. The good news was that the store manager had a policy that employees got a $600 line of credit at the store; you could pay it down with each paycheck. It was good business sense, because you wanted your salespeople to represent the clothing you were selling. I use the lessons I learned then to this day with my own clothing line. In that store I learned how to present myself, how to dress, how to understand basic fashion principles and presentation, negotiate in a sales situation and working with customers. And then when that job was done for the day, I'd go put on jeans and deliver Mazzio's pizza. That job provided many a dinner for me and my sister that summer. I held the Ralph Lauren job through the Christmas holidays and into the next spring.

It was important to just keep pushing forward, putting food on the table and learning whatever I could as I searched for my purpose. Where was I going to end up? My sister had her ambition to be a performer. My football dreams had been, literally crushed. Was I going to be in retail my whole life? Just before Christmas that year, my sister had to drive to New Mexico to help Dad out of a jam. They ended up having to sell the car, so Angelique was stuck there until our Mom sent her a ticket to move to southern California. Since she wanted that singing career, the LA area was a good place for her to be. And still, I stayed on in Tulsa, not clear of where my life was heading, but determined to move forward. Refusing to move forward would be an action statement made through inaction and no one suffers greater from this than our selves. We hurt the core of our being by refusing to strive to fulfill the purpose we've been born to achieve.

The Creator has given each of us a purpose and we must move forward and put action behind our intentions to discover what it is. We have to be willing to first put action and effort behind our hopes and aspirations.

In the spring of 1989, my dad asked me to work with him on the road. By then I was so ready to get out of Oklahoma. And it would be cool to get away and drive all over the country with my Dad. Besides, my plan for life wasn't exactly working out. And so, along with a friend from Mazzio's we hit the road with Dad selling advertising. We traveled all over New Mexico, eastern Texas and Arizona. I didn't think this was going to be my path in life either, but it was a relief to have the freedom this kind of work offered. And though I couldn't know it at the time, it was all basically a training ground for what my life would become.

Pop standing in front of the middle section of his garden. In my dream, Pop talked to me from the rows of corn to the left.

Pop with his siblings- My Great Uncle's and Great Aunt.

Pop and Nan took this photo a few years before their passing.

My high school senior picture.

Pictured here with my girlfriend at our high school prom.

Graduating from high school.

Me with my family, shortly after I graduated from high school.

– Part Three –
Warrior's Road

"Grandson, you have come very far and fought well, you have traveled the warrior road, you have seen many things, some bad more good, I have watched you. Your ancestors see you. Remember your ancestors when you go now. Remember I am with you. fear nothing. I will make your way. Be strong grandson. I am waiting here for you on this side. Aho" LF

Chapter Seven

~ Where there's a will... ~

"See beyond what you think of you and see you as the creator made you!
You are the only one of you...but you must know that."

At twenty years old I hit the road with my Dad. I don't really know what I hoped to achieve. I just knew I had to keep moving, had to make a living and had to see more of the world than Oklahoma. The only way I would have been able to finish college was on a football scholarship. Since the back injury took care of that, I had to find another path. I wasn't afraid of work and I was always open to learning something. With all the different jobs I'd been doing since age sixteen, I was developing a business sense. It wasn't from an accredited university, but I was definitely getting an education working with my Dad as a traveling salesmen.

"Where there's a will, there's a way." I still remember how often my mother would say that. She was now living in California, working at Nordstrom's department store. My sister was living with her, pursuing her dream of being a performer. For me, the will was to keep pushing, to find my own way. And the way before me was to work with my Dad. Although it wasn't the path I felt was my ultimate destiny, it was the path opening for me at the time and so I took it.

I believe that if you yearn to achieve something, you must apply your energy toward accomplishing it or it will never come to you. You have to be willing to get up and walk forward on your path and grow your faith. And as you walk, you will discover that all the things you needed were always ahead of you on your path. You come to know that if you would have stayed where you were and never moved forward, you would have missed out on all the things you needed by waiting for them to come to you. I knew I had to go and search out my path with faith that the resources I would need would be brought forward. It would be from every step of the journey that I would gain the knowledge and wisdom that would prepare me not only to appreciate my blessings but provide the experiences necessary to sustain my path.

At first, Dad was selling advertising inserts that went into the phone book. I learned a lot about communicating with people, how to read people, speak with them. Very quickly, that job ran its course. For a man who had developed three of his own businesses, Dad was getting sick of working for other people. In Albuquerque, he worked with a tire and service garage that did a promotion where the customer purchased a $30 card, which entitled them to free maintenance services worth over $300. We sold this promotion to the public via door-to-door solicitations. Dad thought this was a great promo. He worked there long enough to see how they did it and then moved on and did it himself. He went to Texas and sold the program there. He taught me how to walk up to a complete stranger and walk away with a check. It taught me how to get somebody's attention. Most importantly, it taught me how to get beyond myself.

Personality-wise, I wasn't that outgoing. To walk up to a complete stranger's house and start up a conversation with them took a lot of guts. It taught me how to communicate. It also taught me perseverance. A lot of doors slammed in my face, but it taught me to keep going. You had to believe that the next person might love this.

Looking back on these experiences, I can see how I was learning the importance of presentation, confidence, and promotion. I didn't know how these skills were going to support me in the future, but I was happy to learn their value.

During this same time, my sister was in California living with our Mom and trying to get her singing career started. I took some time off and went out to visit them. Angelique had been telling me about how great her new music producer and recording sessions were. Although I enjoyed music, I really didn't even consider being a performer. But my sister had other plans.

Angelique told me she had a new song and to write a rap for it. She was going back soon to do some recording at her music producers little studio in the Watts section of Los Angeles. It was in a guesthouse in the back her music producer's house. Angelique was one of the few people who had read my poems and stories from my journals. In the days when we were losing everything, in danger of losing the house, I would sit and write. On occasion I would share those very personal writings with her. When she asked me to write something, I figured it was something for her or someone else to perform. So, I wrote this rap.

She liked it and said that they needed me to go in and do a scratch vocal so whoever ultimately performed the rap could hear the flow and cadence of it. I refused. I told her, I wrote it but I'm not performing it. But she and the producer convinced me. So, I stepped into the recording booth, put the headphones on, heard the music and when my part came up I just rapped the verse. And…it was awesome! I don't mean I did an awesome job at it. It was such a momentous experience for me. In that moment, I got bit. I just loved becoming part of the music and letting my voice add to that music. It really, really excited me. I thought…this is incredible! It reminded me of the time when I was eight years old, laying on the floor in my sister's room getting so caught up in my connection to the music and the space inside my heart.

After the first pass, the engineer stopped the tape and said, do it again, put more energy into it, really like, hit certain parts you want to emphasize. I looked at what I wrote in a whole different way, understanding that it's not just the writing, it's how you say it. We did it again. When I took off the headphones, he said, "Ok, that's a keeper – that was hot." I looked over at Angelique. She was smiling one of those "I told you so" smiles. I was pretty sure she planned this from the very beginning when she asked me to write something. The Creator uses all means possible to show us our way. We just have to pay attention.

After that, I started listening to other rappers, studying the artistry of hip hop, being a mc, being a lyricist. It all began with my sister. If I didn't thank her then, I certainly thank her now.

At the time, I knew I liked doing it, but I didn't know how to make money doing it. I loved doing what I did in that booth. I was excited about learning more and became a student of it. I wanted to learn more about how to do it. How do you make a song that moves somebody? It intrigued me how all these energies come together and when it all clicks it's just incredible. The whole process just intrigued me.

At first it was me writing fairly mainstream raps, like the one I wrote for my sister. I hadn't yet put two and two together to see where this was taking me. I was a baby as a songwriter and not even close to being a performer. I didn't have any music. I would have to create things in my head to write. I had beats in my head, but couldn't define the musicality of anything I was writing. So I realized that if I was going to write my own lyrics, I would have to find a way to create the music. So, I worked my butt off to buy a keyboard -- a Yamaha SY77, one of the first "smart" keyboards; kind of a music workstation with a sequencer.

At the beginning, I was trying to find my way and hone my skills. It was important to gather a style and find how I would say what I had to say. That was a huge part; learning how to inject your energy in a way that people hear what you say the way you wanted to say it. I wanted to experiment with writing all kinds of rap songs. When I began to understand that I had a talent for this, it began to hit me: this is a tool, a gift from the Creator. It was important to recognize how to use this.

Looking back now, I can see how my mother's claim back when I turned thirteen was bearing fruit: *"They are plans for good and not for evil. To give you a future and a hope."* But at the time, I just knew that I had found a voice and I had to take responsibility for how I used it. There was a lot I was trying to figure out – a lot of time feeling overwhelmed about all the elements: recording, performing, defining your talent musically, trying to understand the process and technique. I wasn't a prodigy, but I steadily worked at it. I needed to know so much more before I could be sure of myself as an artist.

This lasted for a couple of years – more like a hobby because there was life to deal with – still working. However, I did sense the beginnings of the recognition of a new avenue and purpose. I was having the experience of how *The Medicine of Prayer* was guiding me to find the path I was born to walk. I was learning that when you put YOUR energy into YOUR path you are performing the action that causes the reaction of blessings from the Creator.

Our faith requires works to achieve blessings and prosperity. When we put our works into action the Creator causes us to be rewarded with resources we could never imagine. But we have to be willing through faith to get out there in the garden and get dirty, get sweaty and earn it. When we put forth that kind of energy and effort toward the seeds of our faith, we are showered with blessings. We accomplish things that others did not think possible. We harvest exactly the resources that our destiny calls for and most importantly, needs in order to flourish in this life.

And yet, there are always more lessons to be learned. Just when you think you've learned one thing, you get tested. Kind of like being in school, you know? I think the most challenging lesson of all is understanding the difference between moving forward with what we want versus knowing what it is we need.

At this point, I had turned twenty-one. My sister had put her musical pursuits on hold and moved to Florida with her boyfriend Steve, who had been signed by the Tampa Bay Buccaneers. I was still working with my Dad in Albuquerque and working on developing myself musically. I had been living a wandering kind of existence for a couple of years and wanted to find some security, something stabilizing in my life.

That's when I met a girl and thought this was the kind of stability I was searching for.

Chapter Eight

- Even through the lies... -

"Be encouraged! Funny how the lil voice of negativity can seem so loud. But remember, it's small and you have the Creator of all with you 24/7!"

Over the years, I've learned that sometimes we have to go through difficult things to get clarity. We have to go through pain and upset to appreciate all we've been blessed with. Some people need to experience the lesson over and over. Some learn it the first time. I've always been quick. I've also been a little hardheaded, too. I've had my share of beating my head against a brick wall, thinking that was the way to get to the other side, when really, I just needed to take a few steps to the right, and walk around it. But I knew what I wanted and I'm tenacious.

She worked at the bank where my Dad and I would cash our company checks. You couldn't miss her among all the other tellers. She had been a runner up for Miss New Mexico. By then the sales work had helped me get over my reluctance to talk to strangers. We clicked, we started dating and soon enough we moved in together in Albuquerque. My sister and Steve had married on Valentine's Day 1991. In April that same year I married the girl from the bank. It seemed like our family was finally settling down. It seemed to me that she understood that I was striving to push forward in a music career. And it also seemed that she had faith in my eventual success. I had met the owner of a recording studio in

Tulsa and proposed that we move to Oklahoma for a six-month trial. If I wasn't making any progress with my music after that time, then we'd figure out our next move. Although she wasn't too thrilled about moving to Oklahoma, she agreed.

Obviously, I felt music was what I wanted to do. Upon arriving in Tulsa, I went back to my old business -- mowing lawns. I hustled up some lawn mowing equipment and went door to door asking people if they needed their lawn mowed. Within a couple of weeks I had about thirty lawns that covered our living expenses and gave me the flexibility to go to the studio at night to work on my music. I had rounded up some dancers from the local club scene and each night after recording, I would shift gears and work on dance routines to my songs until the sun came up. This went on all through the summer.

As I continued building my skills, I knew I needed a professional name. Rapper Gary Paul wasn't going to cut it. I went over name after name in my head for several days, but none seemed right. The name finally came to me at a pow wow in Pawhuska, OK -- Osage country. I was sitting in the stands listening to the winners of the pow wow being announced. There was a grass dancer there who won, whose surname was Lightfoot. That was it.

At that time, dancing was very prevalent in hip hop – it was an integral part of a performance. All my songs had a choreographed dance routine to them. When I heard that name, I thought wow, that's something that would work. Out of respect for the Lightfoot family, I decided to spell the name a different way. Over time, the name has taken on more meanings. In one song lyric I talk about being light on your feet, another suggests I shouldn't be taken lightly. At the same time the name incorporates the message of having clarity, of always being able to see your path clearly. And so I had my professional name -- Litefoot.

It took nearly the entire six-month "Oklahoma" trial period for me to get my first professional concert booking. The Alpha Phi Alpha fraternity on the University of Oklahoma campus hired a number of bands and artists to perform at a party they were throwing during homecoming weekend. It was my first paid performance and I was ecstatic. I left Tulsa early and headed for the OU campus outside of Oklahoma City for my first real sound check and rehearsal. I didn't go on until about nine or ten at night and she was going to meet me there after she got off work. This was the big night, when everything was finally coming together. I had done it! It had been a hard road all these months, but now I could see it all paying off. There were some fairly established groups there, but, I was still trying to get my break.

As time passed, I kept looking for her to arrive. Soon it was time to go on and still I didn't see her. I was a little worried. Not only had she not arrived, but some of the groups that went on before us got booed off the stage. They had stuff thrown at them. This was like being at the famed Apollo Theatre in Harlem where if you weren't good enough the audience would let you know in a New York minute. I was thinking, I'm going on after these guys…what are they going to do to us? The best thing about that night was that I was the only artist that didn't get chased off the stage. I found that I could hold my own in front of an audience. I was a hit!

After the show, I realized that she had never showed up. Now I was really getting worried. There was no answer at the house. I even called the police to see if they could do a check of our apartment, just to make sure nothing was wrong. Finally, I called her mom. I told her I was at the show and I couldn't find her. And then, in a very matter of fact tone, her mom told me the news: *she's left you...you'll find a note when you get to the apartment.* Just like that, it was over.

By this time, it was past midnight. I didn't go back to Tulsa that night. I was basically in a state of shock. Like I was in some horrible nightmare I couldn't wake up from. The show was incredible and well received. There was so much positive energy and then, within hours of that success to be blindsided by betrayal and negativity. I had known this was a pivotal time in the relationship. It was critical for me to prove that my goals weren't just a fantasy and would succeed. This night proved, to me at least, that I could hold my own in front of an audience. It was forced upon me to recognize in that point and time that a lasting relationship with her was not going to happen.

When I did return to the apartment in Tulsa everything was gone. I mean, the place was cleaned out -- furniture, appliances, dishes. She left only my clothes, the two champagne glasses from our wedding and a note. Afterward, we had one or two conversations, but she wasn't having it. We had been married less than six months so it wasn't even necessary to get a divorce – the marriage was annulled. That was appropriate because an annulment means the marriage is null and void, as if it had never even happened. Marriage is a union, a promise of support, fidelity and trust. Clearly, that never existed as far as she was concerned. Understanding that the annulment was for the best didn't stop me from becoming really depressed. The situation had spun my world around. I had hit rock bottom.

There was no way I could stay at the empty apartment. My sister and her husband had moved back to Tulsa and they took me in. Once again, I was homeless, transportation-less, single and my seasonal lawn work had all dried up. I was sleeping on the couch at my sister's apartment wondering what could possibly be my next step. This went on for nearly two weeks. On one of those days, I was sitting there in one of my abandoned doldrums, stuck on the couch. There was a television special or documentary on about the Battle of Little Big Horn.

The life of Crazy Horse had always been a recurring theme to me. I remember being very impacted by the belief and sense of purpose I saw through the storytelling about these great warriors. And it started me to think – who are these people today? Who are the people who would be our Crazy Horse right now? Who are the people willing to make our communities the number one priority? Who did I know? Where were these people who could stand up and make a difference?

You know of the few people in your tribe or here and there in organizations like the American Indian Movement. But where are the people nationwide that are icons? It was disturbing to me to think about this man who gave his life to ensure that Native people would have a better future and I had to ask myself, what had we done with that sacrifice? What had we done to achieve his vision of what could be done? What could I do?

I realized how little energy had been put into Indian people to have a presence. I began to realize that the best usage of my talent would be dedicated to the people. Dedicated to my family and their struggle. To my grandfather and all that he had overcome as a Cherokee man. I mean, if I was going to really do this music thing, I could do it in a way that used my talents to transcend music. It couldn't just be about me getting even with my ex by proving that I was right and could succeed. It had to be more expansive than just avenging the betrayal I'd been dealt.

Sitting Bull had said: *"Let us put our minds together and see what kind of life we can make for our children."*

I began to really feel that this was the way my gift could be best used. I didn't know of anyone else who was doing that. It could have an incredible impact.

Rap music had become a powerful international musical force. It was a medium that allowed people to give voice to social issues; at its best, it was a musical form that educated young and old alike about the world around them. It gave a voice to the voiceless. The direction I was considering to pursue with my music was the beginning of my evolution of becoming a Native rapper.

There is an incredible lack of information about our people in the mainstream. Why couldn't I rap about Native culture and Native people and our experiences? And who's to say I couldn't rap about other things? Obviously, music from a rap artist is supposed to be about their life and about who they are. I was beginning to put all of the pieces together and they were giving me my direction. It just kept coming to me to be a voice. To fill a void that had for too long been left empty. These days, there are rappers on almost every reservation in North America – but not back in 1991.

This was a defining moment that played on me as I evaluated my life and my music. Why couldn't I be a Native American rap artist that had appeal to the world? Why couldn't I say something? I was looking around and wondering, how come we're not in magazines and on the radio? How come we can't be Indian people and be seen on television living the way we are today? We are still alive and exist. All I saw in mainstream media were images of us from the past, riding horses, living in teepees. I began to feel this fire burn. Who says I couldn't do something to change that? Instead of waiting for somebody – I'm somebody. My Dad wasn't too optimistic about the whole thing. He still hoped I could find a way to pursue my original goal of becoming a lawyer. But I was too full of piss and vinegar to think I couldn't do it.

Why couldn't this happen? I didn't know if anybody would like it, but this was how I could express myself. I believed my talents and abilities would be able to make an impact, but did I know that for sure? It would take a lot more faith. I didn't know of anyone in Indian Country at the time that was out doing something in entertainment like what I was envisioning. I believed the world and, most importantly, Indian country needed somebody like that.

In many ways, Native people are probably the only people that have to first educate the majority of mainstream society in order for them to understand and appreciate us as artists or as modern day people in today's world. And I think that's a very unique and unfortunate situation.

The fault, to some degree, falls on us because we have not been able to express ourselves in the same way as many other races of people in this country have found to do. In one regard the fault may rest with us, as we have in many ways embraced the stereotyping and romanticizing of our culture that has come at the hand of our oppressor. At the same time it's really not a fault of ours in the sense that we didn't ask for the history that was bestowed upon us. We've done our best to deal with it and to move forward in this country with that history.

Something I've experienced is the necessity to always have to explain 'why' and 'how come' about Native people. I am often in the position of having to give others a context of understanding Native people before they can even see you as a rapper or see Native people as doctors or lawyers, because society is most comfortable seeing Native people in beads, buckskins and leathers. Outside of that, there really is no bridge for others to connect because they're really not aware of the modern day situation of Native Americans.

It was definitely time for me to pray. And it was through *The Medicine of Prayer* that I was able to get back on my feet. I began to accept the reality of the break-up. I would need to have enough faith to let that door close.

If I wasn't going to chase after her, then I needed to know that pursuing the music was what I was meant to do. I was praying a lot of the time to be clear about my purpose, to know if this was what the Creator had for me to do. If this was something that was good, then let me continue to do this.

Ironically, it was the moment when I found out she bounced, that a music career became really real. When she left I had nothing and music became that replacement. At the same time I was miserable. The music gave me an outlet for dealing with the breakup. I dove into working. The busier I stayed the less I had time to think about it. Thinking about it just wasn't good for me.

After a couple of weeks, my brother-in-law had a long talk with me about "getting back in the saddle." I had to do something for work and he offered me a suggestion. He worked as a supervisor at Miller Brands and he could talk to them about getting me a job. They were really serious about the equal opportunity thing and keeping within the corporate compliance guidelines. So, being Native American there might be a spot for me. It may not be the best job, but it was a job. I had no problem with that. In any case, my brother-in-law ended up being my boss.

My job was to go to different grocery stores and do merchandising. I was responsible for making sure all the products were filled up, all of the shelves were stocked, the products were faced with labels forward, point of sale, displays, marketing materials, basically ensuring that all the Miller products were in place and available for the customer. Again, this job would help me later on in my music career by helping me understand both branding and marketing.

The really beautiful thing about the job was that after a month, I learned to do all my work, which started at 5:30am, and complete my route in half a day. I would then go back home and go to sleep for about four hours, get up and go punch out. Then off to the studio all night. Since I had made the decision to continue pushing my music career forward, when I got done with work, I was in the recording studio every single night.

So that became my routine – work all day and record all night. The guy working with me at the studio was on time sometimes but most of the times I waited an hour or more for him to show up. On those occasions, because he was late to the studio, I only got an hour of sleep before work began at 5:30 in the morning. But I kept pushing forward. Finish up work in the morning, come back home and sleep from noon till 4:00 P.M., punch out and then back to the studio. If I didn't do it nobody was going to do it for me.

It wasn't always easy, and I did have detractors. What I was trying to do had never been done. Hip hop and rap had come out of the black community and here I was, a Native trying to jump into an already crowded market. I was told by my local hip hop competitors to give it up. Indians beat on drums and ride horses, they'd say. Indians don't rap. Comments like that only served to make me more determined. But to be honest, there would be times when I questioned myself, too. I was dreaming big. Was it too big? Was I setting myself up for failure? These kinds of aspirations weren't encouraged in Indian Country. Just get enough education to get a job, don't drink and stay off drugs was where the bar had been set… or rather stuck.

There was a moment during this struggle when I seriously wondered about what I was trying to accomplish. It had been a hard day and I was sitting outside on a hot summer Oklahoma night. I was still living with my sister and her husband. Through the open window, I heard them talking. My brother-in-law was concerned, feeling that I was wasting my life and needed to get a real career. Maybe go back to school and get my degree, he offered. My sister defended me and though I knew it wasn't meant for me to hear, it did hurt. I also knew that his words came from a place of genuine concern.

Friends and family had confronted me with everything from *"you know how our Indian people can be…"* to *"you're gonna dedicate your whole energy and life for people who might spend more time tearing you down and not lifting you up."* I was told of the pitfalls of Indian Country; the politics and in fighting and back-stabbing. And that advice wasn't wrong. It was and is a very real element in any oppressed community – where the oppressed become the oppressors. I was encouraged to go back to school, to reconsider spending so much time doing this because ultimately, people weren't going to appreciate it. I know for sure that my family didn't want to see me getting hurt. I didn't take it personal. In fact, there's nothing like somebody telling me I can't do something to spur me on.

There was something my father told me once that pushed me forward. He said: "You know why somebody with less talent and less ability achieves greatness? Because they don't know that they can't." There's a lot to be said for purpose and perseverance. Coupled with the Creator it becomes a force.

Things started to move. I was performing in any local rap contests that came up. I was a regular performer in all the clubs and getting good response. My music was speaking to people. One of my earliest hits, "The Money" had just won a local rap search contest. One night a DJ at the most popular radio station, K107 came to the club where I was performing. The surprise was that the DJ was a guy I'd gone to school and played football with. I had no idea he had become a DJ or had any interest in music.

The miracle was that not only did he happen to be at the club, but he saw my show and we connected. He loved my music, telling me that it was as good as anything he was playing during his evening radio show. He was saying, "Man, why aren't you playing this on the radio?" At the time, my understanding of the business was that in order to get radio play, you needed to supply a lot of under the table cash to the radio station or be tied to a major record label. I had neither of those things back in 1992. But the DJ was determined to get me on the air. There was a segment on the radio called "Hot or Not" where the DJ put on a song and listeners would call in and vote on whether the cut was hot or not. He decided my song, "The Money" had to be included in this segment.

When he played "The Money" on air the first time, people loved it. It got call after call – hot, hot, hot. When I came into work the next day, people had heard it on the radio the night before and I felt like a mini-star, like being on national television. The station put it into rotation and it climbed in rank each night on the countdown. The DJ asked me what else did I have, so I gave him another song called, "Speciality" a rap ballad I wrote. People loved that too. It stayed on the countdown for 16 weeks. It sat at #4 behind mega stars and groups for weeks.

I didn't want to be just some kid with a demo. I was trying to do things as professionally as possible and presentation was really important. I learned that from Dad while working with him on the road, selling door to door. I remembered the importance of presentation from the Ralph Lauren store and from all the shelves that I'd been filling for Miller. I had grown up seeing my father run his own companies and that any goal was attainable. I just knew the things I had learned would all need to be put into play now. You can't do all the PR and marketing until you have a brand.

In the midst of this, I got a call at the house. It was someone asking for Litefoot. It was the program director from K107 where my friend the DJ worked. He was calling to congratulate me on the success of the music and the support I was getting. And…this was the shocker…he wanted to let me know that they got a call that day from Jive Records. They were asking about this guy Litefoot, who had been taking the 4th spot on the countdown for so many weeks.

Apparently, the radio reps at Jive felt that I was in the way of their artists moving up on the countdown, but they were more impressed by my music and the ability I obviously had to market myself and create a buzz. So, they called the program director to get in contact with me and he wanted to know if it was okay for him to give them my number so they could call me directly. Hmm, let me think – give Jive Records my number? Yeah, I think so.

The call came. I was invited to come to Chicago and meet with the executives at Jive Records about possibly making it my recording home. This was intense. I had just gotten into the whole music aspect. I was the rookie. Other local rappers had warned me, saying I would never get radio time, much less sign a deal with a major record label. But then I did get on the radio and now I was invited to discuss a record deal. It turned out that these local rappers were my first haters. I suppose success was really coming my way.

Being invited to come to Chicago was overwhelming. I decided I would not make the trip alone and invited my dancers and a couple of crew, asking them to come with me. We could drive out together and they could be there with me when I signed my record deal. They had been with me from almost the beginning, so I thought, let's go make this happen and share in the experience.

When we got to Chicago I went to meet with the label rep. They showed me around and took me out and showed me the city. They spared no expense. The next day I went into the meeting. This was the big time. This company had signed the likes of R. Kelly, Q-Tip, and A Tribe Called Quest. If they were making me an offer, I was ready. And they did. The executive told me they were ready to go forward. They wanted to have me do records on their label. So far, so good. If only he had stopped right there and given me the contract. But he had more to say. They wanted my talent, but they didn't want me to rap about my culture or include my Native American heritage in my music in any way.

Needless to say, this kind of hit me sideways. It was stunning to me that he could sit there and think nothing of asking me to drop my identity. I was stunned and really offended that he felt my people's culture or the Native American aspect of my music wouldn't translate to mainstream audiences. I didn't understand how that would be a detrimental thing to my career or alienate non-Native people.

If you look at a lot of rap and R&B that is performed by African-American artists, the majority of people buying the music are non-black. Even when the lyrics overtly denigrate whites – whites still buy the records. I wasn't even going close to that. And my music was obviously popular with Native and non-Native people, that's why it was sitting so long in the countdown. It is why Jive called me. It's why I was in Chicago. I had to ask, how do you figure the original people of this country wouldn't get the same response as other rap artists?

He flat out said, "You have to understand, your people don't buy records. Your people spend money on alcohol. Indian people make up less than half of a half of a percent. So why would you cater your music to a demographic that doesn't exist in any significant numbers?"

It took a whole lot of willpower to not curse this man or use my hands on him. Here I was being told what my people mean from a marketing, corporate point of view.

It really hit me then. I learned a lot very quickly. Here I was ready to sign contracts and make it happen and ended up getting schooled on understanding that the mountain I thought I was ready to climb was way bigger than what I thought. I had already resolved myself that my journey in music was going to be way different from what other artists do, so it didn't take long to give the man my answer.

I told him I really appreciated them bringing me out here and all. But my people, the ones you don't want me to rap about…the one's who don't spend money on records…well, we are in the condition we are today because too many people have signed contracts like the one you're offering. Thank you, but my answer to your offer is…no. I stood up and walked out the door.

That's when I realized that the same passion and perseverance I knew I had, was going to be the main ingredient in accomplishing the things I needed to accomplish in the way I wanted to accomplish them.

A lot was weighing on me as I walked away, because I was really torn. I'd said no thank you based on principle, but from a business point of view I'd just done what most people would call the dumbest thing on Earth. It would not be the last time I would have to walk away from opportunities or events that didn't make sense to others.

Through the Creator we find the strength to stand alone.

Clearly though, if I had signed that contract, there would be no way I could say what I wanted to say, what I felt needed to be said, and what I had committed to do with the gift I was given. The music would immediately be watered down if not rejected by them outright. It's amazing to me in hindsight, because now people see me being successful in a number of things and accuse me of selling out or that I'm rapping on the rez because I couldn't do it globally or get signed to a major label. Little do they know that the biggest sell out I could have taken was offered to me right out of the box by one of the hottest major labels at that time.

After the meeting when I got back outside, the crew was eagerly waiting. They were asking about when I would start recording? When was the first music video gonna be filmed. I just said -- who wants to take the first shift on the drive back to Oklahoma?

After getting back to Tulsa, I rolled my sleeves up and became more determined and focused on achieving my goals. My first order of business was to be able to put my music out on my own label. If a major label was not going to allow me to say what I wanted to say, then I would start my own label, put my music out myself and do it my way. It would also be something I could grow to put out other artists – a label that would serve as a home for other Native talent. Naturally, I needed a distinctive name. I was going need more money too. So I got a second job working at a clothing store in the mall.

There was a popular label at that time called Delicious Vinyl. I associated vinyl as an intricate part of hip hop and then came the idea of it being red and that it was for Native people. I felt like as a Native in hip hop the label I would own would have to incorporate that whole energy. So Red Vinyl Records was born. I went to the bank and opened an account doing business as Red Vinyl Records.

I didn't discuss it with anybody. It was just time to make it happen. From then on all my contracts for concerts and speaking engagements all carried the name of my new label. It was the brand that I would promote all over the country. But first it would all have to come together in Oklahoma. I was ready to bring Litefoot and Red Vinyl Records to every Indian Community in my home state.

The momentum with the music was growing and I began to perform all over Oklahoma for different tribes and communities. It wasn't always easy to convince Indian communities to book me. I would take the heat for gangsta rap and some of the lyrics and stereotypes of rap at that time – that it was edgy, controversial and scary. Initially, there was a fear that by me coming to the community, especially in remote areas, my music would incite things. I had to take the time to educate about what I was about and that not all hip hop artists rap about the same things.

It was during this time that I made up my mind to request a meeting with Chief Wilma Mankiller, the Principal Chief of the Cherokee Nation of Oklahoma. I wanted to let her know about the message I was trying to get across with rap music. I didn't know what to expect, but I was honored when she asked me to come perform as her guest at a high school. She also asked me to give a short speech after my performance. This I really did not expect. I let her know that I would be happy to perform my music and say something. Yet, in my mind I wasn't so sure about the whole short speech thing. I had never considered speaking as part of my performance. But I was not about to deny the request. Even though I didn't feel I was competent or experienced in giving short or long speeches, I had to have faith that the words would come. And so I humbly accepted the invitation from my Chief.

On the day of the performance, when it came time to speak, I could only send up a prayer to the Creator that I speak the words that needed to be spoken. I didn't try to write a speech. I sent up the prayer, and let go. When I finished talking people stood up clapping. I thought they were clapping for Chief Mankiller, and turned toward her as she came on stage and began clapping, too. She indicated that the ovation was for me. I can honestly say I was amazed that the applause was for what I had said. That moment let me know that by having total faith, the Creator will show us what we are meant to do and give us the way to do it.

After that first talk at the high school, I started receiving more support from many Cherokee communities. One of my first and longest lasting supporters is Lisa Trice, who at that time was the reigning Miss Cherokee. She was working for the Cherokee Nation and helped facilitate events for Cherokee Nation youth. She saw how my music and talks could reach the youth and became a big supporter of the message and how I was delivering it. She became a very strong advocate and to this day, Lisa and her family remain close dear friends of mine.

Lisa was instrumental in booking my first big conference. It was all older people, but she was convinced that if I showed them what I was doing it could set in motion my movement from tribe to tribe throughout Oklahoma. She helped get me booked to perform at the Johnson O'Malley Title V Indian Education Conference being held that year at the Doubletree Hotel in downtown Tulsa. There were Title V Coordinators there from every tribe in Oklahoma representing thousands of schools where Native students were being served. I'm pretty sure this was the first time 99% of the audience was hearing rap music. But they heard the message in my music too. Again, my music and the unique manner in which I was delivering it began to gain acceptance from elders and those working for change and betterment across Oklahoma. The requests from more and more tribal communities for me to come perform and speak poured in.

Things were happening fast and at times I felt they were going too fast. I was still trying to get used to speaking in front of people. There were times when I didn't feel ready for all of this. I didn't want to accept what I was being called to do and I was resisting it. I could feel the magnitude of the impact all this could have on my life and the people around me, and that scared me. I was realizing the truth of being careful about what you ask for when you're praying.

Chapter Nine

– Dream ≈ Commitment –

*"There's power within you...you may have not even begun to extract.
No resource on Earth can do more for guiding and sustaining you
than your spirit."*

I was more dedicated to pursuing my music and growing Red Vinyl Records than ever before. I continued to work my job at Miller and my second one at the mall. And I was also working harder than ever in the studio. I was burning the candle from both ends and it really felt like it too. It was exhausting work. I was now traveling to perform and speak at events all over Oklahoma but had to keep both my job's to pay for all the expenses associated with a fledgling upstart record label. Juggling it all was a challenge and I often took turns with my dancers driving through the night, getting from a show back home in time for work -- catching whatever sleep I could on the road. Not everyone could see the potential or felt that all the work was worth the trouble.

But, all my efforts were paying off. I was touring and honing my abilities as a live performer while spreading my message. I was becoming a better rapper and my music was getting better too. I was also becoming a more creative and diverse lyricist. Clearly, I could make hot music. But I also wanted to make the kind of music that spoke to my people and really meant something to Native people everywhere. Mind you, when I was talking about including Native music into hip hop music I would get this blank kind of stare from music producers. I wanted to develop my own sound and represent my culture through my music. I was making good on the stand I took back in Chicago.

There were times when I second-guessed myself on that choice. Could I have signed that contract and established a track record and then moved into more socially conscious music? Maybe I could do it their way only for, let's say a year and then... But I knew better than that. If I had started down their road, I would have had to stay on it because they were paying the bills and I would have truly sold out. The music business is cold. It's rough and spits out artists on a dime. There were not only the usual barriers of trying to succeed, but also racial barriers.

In hip hop, if you weren't African-American what are you doing rapping? This was way before artists like Big Pun, Eminem and Pitbull diversified hip hop and proved that any artist who was dope as an MC could sell platinum and be openly received by the hip hop community. There was a tremendous amount of fighting when I was coming up that still exists today.

In order to get through it, I had to learn to trust the Creator to fight my battles for me.

For me the music business was solely the means for me to achieve what I felt led to do. My purpose was the message; the music was just the vehicle to get that message across. I found myself up against so many who didn't want to believe, who questioned or couldn't see the vision. I could only measure my success on whether or not the message was getting across every time it was delivered. The music broke down the barriers and by the middle of the show people wanted to hear what I had to say.

The message was, as I understood it then, knowing that prayer was a solution to our problems because of who we were as a people. Prayer was at the essence of our core values as Native people yet it was a truth relevant to all people. It is the foundation upon which all human beings are built. Prayer in all of its manifestations is the way we communicate with the Creator and feed and nourish our spirit. It's the base building block in our spiritual DNA. I overcame the difficulties a lot of people have in communicating a message simply because of the way the message was presented. And people were in fact being inspired by it. So I pressed on.

There came a turning point in my journey, when I was really struggling. When I was really at the point of do I go left or go right? Which way am I gonna go? It was a time when I was resisting what I was being called to do. It was all overwhelming for me. I certainly didn't have the answers for curing Indian Country. I was very aware that the problems in Native communities were multi-layered. We were first in all the negative categories: alcoholism, diabetes, teen suicide, drug use, violent crime, domestic abuse. When I did shows, I also spent time with the people afterwards. I heard their stories and saw the living conditions. You could sometimes literally feel the weight of people's despair. I realized again, be careful what you ask for when you're praying because the Creator is listening.

One night, on my way home from work, the weight of this effort was particularly heavy on my mind. Maybe I was fooling myself. Maybe all the naysayers were right and I should go back to school, be a lawyer or something professional like that. I had become so torn and hesitant to do anything more. The hurt I had experienced from the loss of my marriage was still fresh in my mind and I was painfully aware that my getting married was something that was the result of doing what I wanted to do with my life. My being a hardhead and stubbornly doing what I desired in life had cost me a lot. I had no desire to make that mistake anymore. I wanted to be absolutely sure that I was now doing what I was born to do with my life.

I pulled into the parking lot of a convenience store and called my friend, Lisa Trice on the pay phone. I was able to share with her from my heart and she said, just pray about it, ask to be shown. Right then, I put the phone down and prayed. I asked the Creator to please give me the knowledge beyond a shadow of a doubt – is this what you want me to do? Please show me! It was the most sincere prayer I could have prayed.

When I walked in the house that night there was nobody downstairs. I walked into the living room and turned on the TV. Some inspirational program was just beginning. I was about to turn the channel when I heard the announcer say that the program was being broadcast live to Tulsa, Oklahoma from Ontario, California, the very city and state where I was born. I stopped when I heard that. I got chills. Then a guy begins speaking about every question, every hang up that had been going through my mind. He was talking about being called to do something, when you are shown that your path is waiting for you. That your path is older than you are. That when you have this put in front of you either take it and be blessed or you have the choice to walk away. He said we are all born to do something with our lives. When it comes, claim it and move forward. I started crying right there on the couch.

Some people might call that coincidence -- to send up a prayer and then have a seemingly clear answer from a random television program. At the time, I didn't debate it. I remember feeling so exhausted and so overwhelmed that I just ended up falling asleep right there on the couch. I woke up later and there was "snow" on the televsion screen. Yes, in those days, programming actually ended late at night. I couldn't find the channel or anything about the show. Had I dreamed this? Did that really just happen? And so I prayed again. I prayed to please show me…please guide me, give me the strength to do what you have me on the Earth to do. I got up from the couch and went to bed.

Now, I'm not the kind of a person that can get up in the morning if there's not an alarm. It was very late and I had to get up at like five in the morning, to get to work. That night I was just so wrapped up and caught up in this whole effort of figuring out where this was all coming from that I just fell asleep. I was so distraught, that I just didn't do anything normal, didn't set the alarm clock, just laid down and closed my eyes.

The next thing I knew, I was sitting in this field. There's all this tall golden blonde grass that's blowing, and it's real. I'm really there. I can smell the air and the wind. I was there. And when I really kind of took in where I was and began to look around I could see that I was at the base of this hill. I started to see some motion, something coming over the top. First it was a head, the body of a person, coming over the top of that hill. It was daytime and the more that I could see in the distance of who it was, it turned out to be me.

That freaked me out. I'm like, why am I…wait a minute. I'm sitting here and I'm looking at me coming over this hill. As I began to see more of that body come over, I saw there were two young children on each side of me. I was holding their hands walking over that hill. As I began to walk down that side of the hill to where I was sitting, I was raised up in the air and was looking down at myself, watching myself with the children, walking to the bottom of the hill where I would meet me.

Then I realized that I must have moved to the top of the hill. I was still looking down at me, still sitting there and me standing in front of me with the children. I was trying to take it all in and understand it. What did it mean? Then I turned to look over the backside of the hill and it was amazing. I saw multitudes of Indian people, for as far as I could see, moving, walking, coming up over that hill. And I woke up. I woke up and sat straight up in bed.

At first I couldn't breathe, like the air was knocked out of me. But it was just the opposite. When I woke up and sat straight up I wasn't breathing out, I was breathing in. I woke up taking a breath. In many traditions, this is understood as your spirit returning to your body. It goes, it travels to wherever it needs to go and then it comes back. And I remember that moment of sitting straight up, my breath returning to my body and I just began to cry.

It was in that moment something happened that I knew would change my life forever. What I wanted from that point on was no longer relevant. It was about what I had to do on this Earth...to begin to enact what I dreamt onto this Earth to the best of my ability. And I just...I just started weeping at the power of this experience. It was the closest thing that I can ever explain to being with the Creator and feeling that power, that strength. And there are no words for it.

One time I read about how Crazy Horse was, at a certain point in his life, living more on the other side then he did on this side. He knew. Many have known. Once you've been over there, you really want to stay and bask in the power, the peace and the serenity of it all. Words cannot describe the magnificence and the majesty of it. You realize that your time here on this Earth is about trying to live in a good way just to get back there again, to feel that again. Once you know that it exists and how immeasurable it is – there is no denying your connectedness beyond the reality of this world. You understand how small and insignificant we are and how mighty the Creator is. Things fall into perspective very quick.

At the end of the day, I just told the Creator, in the dark, in my room: "I'll do whatever it is you have for me to do. I will run my path and never walk. I will give all to my journey and do the work you have for me." I humbly stated in the darkness that I did not know how nor was I smart enough to know all of the answers to the questions before me. But I committed to the Creator that I would dedicate my life to doing what it is that I was born to do here on Earth.

I didn't want to tell anybody at first. I just took another deep breath, recognizing that I had just returned from a sacred and divine journey. I was filled with humility. I believed that I had been in the presence of the Creator and, like I had prayed, I knew I was on the path I was meant to travel. I had been shown beyond a shadow of a doubt. And when I woke, don't you know, it was the exact time to wake up and get to my job.

There was no time to sit at home and savor this experience. When a prayer is answered in such a powerful way, you get moving. I went to my job, intent on figuring out how I was going to take on the real work of my life full time. My mind was spinning and I was still in awe of all I had been shown. I began my route that morning with an assuredness of my future and a peace that I had never known up to that point in my life. As usual, I'm bringing in the product at one of the stores. There was a guy who always teased me about my aspirations. He worked for a different company, so I didn't always see him. He was there that day and came up to me, smiling in a more than usual bright manner. He said, "Man, I was hoping I would see you. I had a dream about you last night. You're gonna make it!" Now, coming off the dream I'd had, I was not in the mood for his kidding around. But he kept going. And he proceeded to describe to me my own dream.

"I don't know what you were doing, man, but you were out in this field and there were more Native people than I ever seen in my life. I don't know if you were doing a video or concert but there were all these Native people. You're gonna make it!" I nearly dropped everything I had in my hand.

Be careful what you pray for – the Creator is listening.

I had asked to be shown beyond a shadow of doubt, if this was the path for me on this Earth. I got my answer not once, not twice, but three times. It was time for me to move forward – beyond a shadow of a doubt. I could either do the work and become a servant and begin to accomplish my mission or walk away from it. But I had already made my commitment – and in faith I would move forward and fulfill my purpose on this Earth.

It was time now to put action behind my faith.

Chapter Ten

- Prayer in the Desert -

"The greatest test of faith is to believe.
It is the foundation to all the Creator has for you.
Exercise your faith and you exercise life! Pray!"

It is truly amazing and humbling when you begin to see how the Creator moves in your life. Not only was I given clear confirmation regarding the direction of my journey, I could also see how I'd been prepared to carry it forward. As I worked on my game plan, I realized how all the tools I would need were already in my hands. Growing up, going through all the drama in high school, all the odd jobs, all the lessons of those years were now coming into play. At that time, I was simply moving through life as best I could, doing what needed to be done.

Looking back, I could see the power of my mother's claim for me on my 13th birthday: "For I know the plans that I have for you. They are plans for good and not for evil. To give you a future and a hope." Knowing for certain my journey was gathering momentum, I reached for the lessons I learned in the garden with my grandfather about what it meant to be Cherokee. And I put into play everything I learned about marketing, presentation, communication and salesmanship from the jobs I'd had in retail at Ralph Lauren, facing product and point of sale with the Miller Company and the confidence needed to do sales while traveling with my Dad. The lessons of perseverance and discipline I learned while playing football came to my aid. Even the roll up your sleeves sweaty hard work I did while mowing lawns taught me that no job is beneath me. It was like I had been in training all those years for what I was about to do.

In the days after receiving the answer to my prayer, I focused all of my energy and expertise into moving forward in earnest. Prayer without follow through is pointless. The Creator gives the guidance and it's up to us to move on it and make it happen by our actions. Yes, I was shown that I could succeed, but not by sitting at home waiting for a fairy godmother or something. Within days, I compiled a list of addresses for every tribe in America. I wrote an introductory letter about who I was and about my message. I included that information along with a tri-fold brochure stating that I was available for performances and speaking engagements. Every tribe in the United States got one in the mail.

Within two weeks I had booked enough shows that I put in my two-week notice on the job. A month later I was on my way to Maine and the Passamaquoddy Tribe. My journey had truly begun.

When the message first started getting delivered on a broader scale, I was working my way through it, knowing that every one of the problems people were facing in Indian communities had sub problems which then had more sub problems. It was very overwhelming to me to know how to deal with it all. The vision in my dream had only answered my prayer of whether or not this was my path. It hadn't told me how to solve the problems of Indian Country. When I would travel to reservations outside of Oklahoma and hear the things I heard, it definitely had an affect on me. It couldn't help but come out in what I wrote about and spoke about. It made me angry about the past and current government's handling of all things Native. It really made me upset that the current state of affairs in Indian country had never been remedied.

As I traveled, I recognized that a lot of the self-inflicted problems I had seen in my own family I now saw all around the country – the same problems from rez to rez. I could feel the weight of this endeavor. I began to realize how much it would require of my life and the difficulties I would face trying to make a difference in Indian country. All I knew was to reach for *The Medicine of Prayer* once again.

My prayer to the Creator was to give me the words and "get my back" and help me. I didn't know which way to go but I promised to go. All I asked was for the Creator to protect me while I did the work. I told the Creator the night of my dream that I didn't know how to do this. I told the Creator: "I'm going to show up, but you're going to have to guide me."

The whole deal with seeing the people coming over that hill behind me... I didn't know exactly what that meant. I just knew that I'd been given something to do and literally within just a few weeks, I was done working jobs and doing what I'd been doing. I was now out there taking what it was the Creator gave me and put inside of me and spreading it throughout Indian country.

And I can say with certainty that everything that I've been able to do since is because I've always listened to what the Creator has had for me to do. And even though in the last two decades I haven't always had the answers or I've been unclear and was trying to figure it out, the only thing to do was to be still and listen to what the Creator was leading me to do. It's just truly been through the Creator always being there for me, that I've been able to be anything on this Earth. It's so clear and it hurts me to see people out there struggling. They don't realize that they have this source within them and that the Creator cares for them just as much as any of us; that none of us are put above anyone else. It's hard to see people go through that.

So at the end of the day, it's not even a question of "What do I do?" or "Is it ever too hard for me?" It's never too hard, no matter how hard it gets, to stand up and continue to do what it is I know I'm here on this Earth to do. I truly know the Creator is always with me. I know that the blessing of my dream is powerful and I try my best to keep my promise to the Creator every day. Sometimes people get upset at me, telling me to eat, get some sleep. But I never forget my commitment to the Creator. And I didn't say I was going do it whenever I felt good. Or, I didn't say I was going do it whenever everything was beautiful and the timing was perfect. I said I would do it no matter what. And I would run and I would never walk. And when I couldn't run anymore, I would crawl. When your spirit is strong, your body will do whatever the spirit leads it to do. I would do whatever I had to do to never give up on this effort. All I ask is to please show me, give me the things in front of me, because, I don't know. And each time it's shown, it just humbles me more and more and more and more. And I'm blessed, man. I'm blessed.

On my way to Maine, I remember sitting on that plane, traveling to see my people, to do something positive. It was an amazing moment to see what others thought might not even be possible to pursue being fulfilled. I was witnessing the rewards for putting action behind my belief and faith. And not only was I invigorated by what was transpiring before me but my critics and all the naysayers were silenced. At that time, in 1993, there was no such thing as nationwide tours of Native American artists. There were no Natives in tour busses or in any other kind of vehicle going from rez to rez. There were no efforts to reach out to our people nationwide, on all of our different reservations.

The artists during that time were great, but there wasn't a focus on going to reservations. There were no big casinos and nothing financially lucrative about traveling to remote and often times impoverished destinations. In fact, for those who had enjoyed success of any sort outside Indian Country, there was a sense that they had escaped the rez, so why go back there? I'm not blaming anyone here. It's just the way that it was.

A few years later, after I had achieved some success in music and in films, I was at a pow wow on a reservation in Montana. It was the dead of summer, hot and dusty. I was sitting at my booth and this little kid, maybe only six years old, came up and asked, "Are you Litefoot?" I said, yeah, I'm Litefoot. And this kid looked at me, clearly not believing me. I'll never forget what he said. "You're not Litefoot. If you really was Litefoot, you wouldn't be out here." And he turned and ran away. When did we start teaching our young people that once you achieve something you're supposed to walk away and not come back?

That first trip to Maine confirmed how vital it was for me to show up, in person and offer my gifts. I still hold great memories of being welcomed by the Passamaquoddy. Especially the lobster! To them, eating lobster was as normal as hot dogs to the rest of us. They brought me the whole lobster and I didn't even know how to eat it. I just took in every moment and simultaneously was humbled that the Creator was the reason I was experiencing these things. The Creator had provided the vision that this was all possible. He already had blessings in store for me that I had never even contemplated. You begin to understand that the Creator doesn't just want the best for you. He wants the very best for you. The more you walk your path and are blessed by the results of your prayers and living in faith, the more you become humbled by the Creator of all things.

I started out with a black Jeep Cherokee, pulling a trailer with sound equipment, a few t-shirts and pictures. Yeah, kind of ironic, right? I ended up using a vehicle that co-opted the name of my tribe for marketing, and we didn't even get paid for it. We didn't even get asked for permission. I eventually drove the transmission out of that Jeep Cherokee in a blizzard in Wyoming. Who knew that more than a decade later, Jeep would become one of the sponsors for my nationwide Reach the Rez concert and speaking tour by donating a new Jeep Commander? I guess the Creator does have a sense of humor.

Even though things were pushing forward in a positive way, I was still dealing with doubts from others. What kept me going was finding strength in prayer and the certainty of purpose. Bookings were happening throughout Indian country.

It wasn't always possible to set the dates and locations in a reasonably logistical fashion. We had to go when tribes had events, so sometimes there might be a youth conference in Washington and then in two days we would need to be in Nevada for a pow wow and then a day after that in Milwaukee for a music festival. I had a small crew, and we all did a lot. I mean a lot of driving, a lot of loading and unloading of equipment, setting it up and tearing it down. It was hard work. I was making just enough money to pay my crew and get from place to place. We were always grateful when we got fed a home cooked meal. It was a nice change from fast food for breakfast, lunch and dinner.

In addition to the grueling pace on the road, it was challenging to face all the struggles within the communities I was visiting. Fortunately, I was able to express my feelings through music and an unyielding determination to keep moving. And it was always uplifting to be with the people. After a performance the flood of smiles, hugs and requests for autographs renewed my strength and kept me constantly connected to my purpose. That was the wind in my sails.

A fond memory I have is of a grandma at Pine Ridge who came up to me once after a show. She said to me, "Did you see me up there at the front of the stage?" And I said, yeah. And she goes, "Did you see me dancing?" And I said yeah. I told her I was trippin' out because as a grandma she was screaming and dancing as much as the kids were. And then she said to me, "You know why this was so cool for me tonight?" I said, how come? And she told me, "Because when I was these kids age, there was nothing ever like what you did here tonight out here on this reservation. So tonight, at my old age, I had this experience for the first time right along with these kids."

We never know what blessings the Creator has for us or all the many ways that our path could bless other people. That is why it is so important for us all to do what the Creator has for us, because the journey does not end and the path always helps more than just ourselves. And sometimes we have to do things because they need to be done and it is what the Creator has for us to do. This is a test of faith…to show the Creator that we are willing to put our entire trust in our path and through our actions demonstrate that. The Creator will take care of us always. Soon, my own faith would be tested.

I continued traveling and making good on my promise to the Creator to spread the message. I was now receiving write-ups in Indian Country Today newspaper and dozens of tribal magazines and newspapers across the United States. The word was getting out and not long after that the American Indian College Fund contacted me, offering me a spot as a headliner for a music festival they were organizing and taking to Rome, Italy. By early 1994, I was on a plane flying across the ocean to Europe. It was surreal to me and again I was humbled by all the blessings that the Creator kept presenting to me on my path.

After returning from Rome my passion and dedication were flying at an all time high! I immediately hit the road and began touring again. I had built up my stamina to endure all the hard work that comes form living life on the road. I kept my head down and focused on the work that I had been tasked with. No tribal community was too far away and no date was too close together, even it meant driving half way across the country in record time to get there. I was, as Pop used to say, "bound and determined, come hell or high water" to make good on my commitment to the Creator. I was no longer running. I was sprinting.

It was now the summer in Arizona. If you've ever been in Arizona in the summer you know how hot and dry it is. To make matters even more challenging, the air conditioning in my vehicle quit. We were in Globe, AZ near the San Carlos Apache reservation and went to the Walmart and bought a cigarette lighter adapter so we could clip three different little fans to the dashboard. Gotta love that Native ingenuity. Although it just blew the hot air around, at least it was a breeze. And with 3 big Native guys in a Jeep, out in the desert, who had been on the road for quite a while, we needed any kind of breeze we could get.

We did the show in San Carlos, AZ. That show was like an out of body experience. It was so hot and I had been traveling so much. A couple of days later we did a show in Fountain Hills at the Ft. McDowell rez, which was outside and again blistering hot. After that show, I was so dehydrated and worn out I remember laying on a speaker, just too exhausted to move. The crew was telling me to get up, we had to get moving. But I needed a minute. I sent up a prayer: please give me something that will allow my body to rest. I've given everything I've got to give. The next stop is checking into the hospital, so please give me time to nurture my body while I continue to do your work. After that, I took a deep breath, got up and got moving.

Again, I couldn't just lie there and wait for relief. I had sent up the prayer and had to have the faith that the Creator was listening. We got on the road again, heading up through Nevada to Oregon. I didn't know how the Creator would respond to my prayer. I just knew I had to keep moving. I knew we had to get from Arizona to Nevada and on to Oregon. And I had to have faith that the means to accomplish it, to sustain me was out there somewhere on the way. So, I kept pushing forward.

When we got to Burns, Oregon, I checked into our motel. I had a show to perform for the Burns Paiute Tribe the next day. I got a phone call from my Dad back in Oklahoma. He was saying something about Paramount Studios calling and they were wanting to talk to me about doing a movie. He told me something about an Indian and a cupboard. I was not in the mood for any kind of jokes. I told him I was very tired and I would call him later. I hung up. The phone rang again.

It was no joke.

Chapter Eleven

- Prayer Fulfilled -

*"Moving forward doesn't begin with a physical action.
Lasting action comes from your spirit inspiring your mind toward what
you were born for."*

In my wildest imagination, I never would have dreamed something like this. For someone who was still getting used to performing and speaking in front of crowds, struggling to make ends meet so that I could drive across the country to whichever reservation booked me, it was beyond my comprehension to think that a major motion picture company was calling me to audition for a movie. Trust me, I had no desire to be an actor.

My feelings about Hollywood movies was far from favorable when it came to the depiction of Native people. I was cautious. But what I was learning more and more every day was to never underestimate the Creator.

Paramount was doing this movie, the casting was being done out of New York City and they reached out to the American Indian College Fund to inquire about any Native acting talent in the colleges throughout Indian Country. Even though I was not a college student, the College Fund was so impressed with my performance in Rome they told Paramount about me. They had given the casting director my name and Paramount called. They wanted to know if I would come to New York City and audition.

To begin with, the title hit me sideways: *The Indian in the Cupboard*? What was that about? I'd never heard of the book, which was supposed to be a children's classic. No way was I going to do this. I didn't recognize this as an opportunity to continue my work. Nothing about this project felt like the answer to my prayers. I was again being stubborn. Without really realizing it, I had in my own mind already established what would be and wouldn't be considered an answer to my prayers. I was learning that the answers to our prayers do not always come packaged in the way that we think they will. We have to admit, we are just not smarter...than the Creator!

Leading up to that prayer in the desert was a lot of struggle. When you're in battle you don't call for help until you really need it. You don't cry wolf. I had given everything I could. I was physically exhausted. I had trouble getting up, so I more or less picked up the phone and made the call to the Creator. And I really believed the Creator heard me and felt confident that I could move forward. And even though I knew it was going to come, I couldn't stop the fight. I had work in front of me that was part of my path. So I put the request in and kept moving.

When that phone call came I didn't realize it for what it was because I was caught up with my concern about really doing things devoutly. I was trying to do things to the very best of my ability -- to stay 100% true to my belief's and principles. It was not to be difficult or about me. It was for the Creator. I was doing things that I hoped were pleasing to the Creator.

Participating in a film about an Indian in a cupboard didn't seem to me to fit the purpose of my journey.

My father was helping out with my bookings at the time and he told me to stop – read this script first and then make a decision. I said okay, send it over...but I'm not going do it. Looking back on it now, you might wonder what in the world was I thinking? Here Hollywood had found me to do this and I wasn't going to take the call? Literally, found me like I was the proverbial, needle in the haystack. Who does this guy think he is turning down Hollywood? All I can say is that when you're called by the Creator you have an incredible sense of purpose and incredible sense of duty. Often others can't understand that. I did my best to live it everyday.

I was a young man, not yet 25 years old. And to some, I'm sure I came off as arrogant and cocky and way too self-assured. But when you know what you're doing, what your mission objectives are, you can speak very clearly about what is relevant to your journey. I'm sure it seemed flat out stupid -- the idea of a guy in a beat up Jeep Cherokee and a trailer running around to reservations that most people don't even know exist, gets a call to read for Paramount Pictures and he says he's not going to do it? This guy must be the most pompous man on Earth. Doesn't he know that people struggle for years for this kind of opportunity in Hollywood and he's saying he's not interested? Well, that was me.

Sometimes when we pray for things we have to be open and moldable and not so caught up in the mission and the goals to be achieved that we become blinded by them. That could ultimately cause us to reject the opportunity right in front of us. So, thanks to the advice of my Dad, I read the script.

It was a lot different than I expected. I saw how it was a story about responsibility and especially liked the scene where the character of Little Bear kicks the teepee asking, "What's this?" In my life I had tried to demonstrate that Indian people were multi-faceted and not the stereotype seen in the movies. When I saw this scene, I thought it was awesome! I could see that this was not the usual Hollywood hype and could be an opportunity to give an accurate portrayal of Native people. After seeing this movie, how many people would have to then question what they know about Indian people? The character that Paramount wanted me to audition for was named Little Bear. He was a man set in his beliefs who feels out of place in the world in which he's been put. I could relate a lot to that. He was not your typical Hollywood Indian -- "We don't ride, we walk." As the first Native American rapper I could also relate to going against the grain -- of not being the expected representation of what the world thought Native people were and are. Little Bear didn't look like all the stereotypical portrayals of Native people in films. Neither did I. His head was shaved, he had tattoos. My head was partly shaved and I wrote rap lyrics and wore hip hop clothing. It finally began to dawn on me that this might be the Creator's gift – his answer to my prayer.

I had prayed for a chance to rest my body so that I could continue my work. What that would require, I had no idea. A vacation? Who had the money or time for a vacation? I had never done any acting and certainly didn't know what it would take to make a movie. But I could see that participating in a project like this would give Native people a positive representation in the media. If it was meant for me to do this project, it would definitely support the work I was doing, both financially and from a public relations point-of-view. Apparently, I had the best agent in the world – The Creator.

I called my Dad and said, how can we make this happen? He called Paramount back and they said: "Come to New York."

We were in Oregon and the audition was in Manhattan. The nearest airport with reasonably priced direct flights was in Seattle, and oddly enough, our next stop on tour was with the Seneca Nation in New York. Coincidence? You could say that.

What I say is that it was more evidence of the power of *The Medicine of Prayer*.

We left Oregon and the crew dropped me off in Seattle. They would drive the Jeep and trailer cross-country, I'd do the audition in Manhattan, then meet up with them and do the show. Maybe I'd get the job, maybe I wouldn't. No matter what, at least I could get some rest on the flight, instead of driving non-stop from coast to coast. Who knew? All I knew was that a path was opening before me, just as it had when I began working to support the family at age fifteen, or going on the road with my Dad after the injury ended my college football career, or when my sister asked me to write something in that recording studio.

And, just like all the other times, throughout my young life, when a new direction beckoned, I took the step forward with faith that there was something waiting for me to support my journey. Just as I prayed to the Creator to give me the words before speaking in front of that high school group, I knew if this job was going to be mine, it would be through *The Medicine of Prayer*.

I flew out of Seattle into a whole new world.

The after football practice team huddle at Tulsa University.

Rockin one of my first shows at a club in Tulsa.

Getting ready for the Alpha Phi Alpha show at the University of Oklahoma in 1991. This evening would prove to be a pivotal moment in my journey.

Being interview by KJRH Channel 2 News after winning the Rap Search contest at the Tulsa Fairgrounds in 1992.

In '92 I booked one of my first shows as an opening act.
The promoters didn't quite get the name right though.

Performing at the Oklahoma City Myriad during halftime for
the Oklahoma City Calvary semi pro basketball team in 1992.

Another show at a club in Tulsa.

Finally got my initials on my own hat. I was applying the knowledge I had gained to brand and market "Litefoot".

Performing at Tulsa Powwow.

My first photo shoot in Oklahoma.

Performing in Tahlequah, Oklahoma.

This picture was taken during my trip to Chicago to meet with Jive Records.

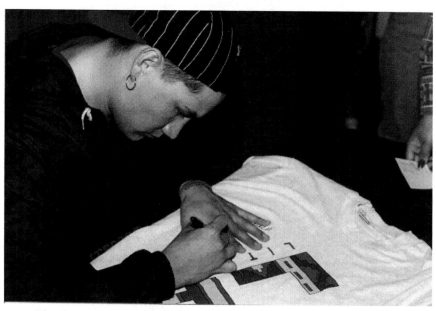

Signing my autograph on a Litefoot t-shirt after a show in Roland, Oklahoma.

Reppin Red Vinyl Records while doing show after show in OK.

In 1993, my good friend Lisa Trice drove me in the Stilwell
Strawberry Festival parade in Stilwell, OK.

Performing at the Tsa La Gi Amphitheater in Tahlequah, OK.

My first performance outside of Oklahoma was in Kodiak, Alaska. It was for an Aleut Elders conference.

Since the beginning I have intertwined Native tradition and culture into my performances. Here I am in Alaska getting ready to do a grass dance exhibition for the people of Kodiak.

My second performance outside of Oklahoma was in
Maine for the Passamaquoddy Tribe.

One of the great memories I have about my very first trip
to Maine was being served a whole Maine lobster.

There is no better feeling than performing from your heart and receiving all that love back from the crowd instantaneously.

Many of the communities where I went had never had concerts before. So much had to be improvised when it came to staging, sound and lights. Here I am in Cherry Tree, OK performing on a tractor trailer pulled in behind a dump truck with cinder block steps up to the stage.

Before I knew it, I was traveling miles all over the United States performing for tribe after tribe. I did most of the driving too.

No matter how long the journey was to get to where I was going or how tired I was… As soon as the show started- the screams and energy from the crowd was just like wind in my sails.

Near San Carlos, AZ doing a photo shoot for Indian Country Today newspaper to accompany a feature story about my music and message.

Receiving special recognition from the Standing Rock Sioux Tribal Council for the message I delivered to the people.

Signing autographs after the show.

Performing in Rome, Italy in January of 1994.

Performing during the summer for the San Carlos Apache Tribe in San Carlos, AZ. It was HOT!

Here's the crowd before my show at the Ft. McDowell Yavapai Nation. This is where I said a prayer after the show, asking the Creator for rest -but in a way that I could continue to fulfill my purpose. The Creator hears our prayers!

Three years after stepping out in faith to follow what I had been led to do with my life, I had kept my promise to run and not walk. To always give one hundred and ten percent. I had no idea that the Creator was about to answer my prayers, *beyond my wildest dreams*!

- Conclusion -

"The Creator is the source of all that I am and everything I yearn to understand & become."

Pray. Listen closely for how the Creator responds. Then move with purpose and enact what the Creator has given you to do. This is *The Medicine of Prayer*. Again, when I am asked how did I get where I am today, I can say with all truth and sincerity that it's all the result of my walk with the Creator. Pray.

Whatever "pray" means to you, that's your business between you and the Creator. Do that. Don't let one more day go by where you don't know why you're here…or just settling for second or third best.

Pray, because it truly indeed is everything that you need. It is where you will begin to find your purpose, what you've been put here on this Earth to do. And it will then become what sustains you as you move forward on that trail, that path, that journey to do what it is you have been put here on this Earth to do. And then you'll understand, nobody can stop you, but you.

The walk with the Creator is truly a warrior's road. Some people have the belief that prayer will make life easy and take away pain and hardship. They look to prayer as some kind of eraser to take away challenges or struggle or to keep bad things from happening. Or people believe that if they pray hard enough, everything they think is broken in their life will be fixed.

My experience of *The Medicine of Prayer* is that it is *walking in partnership with the Creator*. It is being humble before the

Creator and asking for guidance instead of asking for things. It is asking to be shown the purpose for which the Creator has put you on this Earth rather asking to do what you think you want. It is making the commitment to follow the path laid out for you. It is taking action in order to receive all that the Creator has promised. And what you find is that when you are faced with struggles and challenges, you will have the support of the Creator to get through them when you think it can't be done. You will discover the strength, perseverance and patience to live a life beyond what you could ever imagine. You will better understand your place amongst all things.

No matter who you are or from where you come, if you know your purpose and know why you are on this Earth -- and you walk that devoutly, with confidence and with belief every single day – you'll always be able to overcome whatever you or other people may see as insurmountable obstacles. If you're diligent in your belief and in your faith, you will see blessings come your way that no one ever believed possible. When you know your purpose, which comes from the Creator, and when you know that your strength comes from the Creator, in whatever way you pray, stay connected with those two things. Live in this awareness and you will fully understand and be grateful for *The Medicine of Prayer*.

I know this to be true, because it has been and continues to be…the story of my life.

അ

About the Author

Litefoot is an enrolled member of the Cherokee Nation of Oklahoma. He is a Native American rap artist, actor, role model and entrepreneur. Litefoot began realizing his entrepreneurial dreams nineteen years ago by starting his own recording label, Red Vinyl Records and releasing his own music. He has since recorded eleven award-winning albums that have been distributed throughout the world.

Litefoot's lyrics are used today to teach both high school and college level students throughout the United State, and as far away as Germany, about historical and contemporary Native American issues and views. Litefoot has lectured at various colleges throughout the United States ranging from Virginia Polytechnic College and State University to Sitting Bull College. Litefoot spends a great deal of his time each year speaking and holding workshops for elementary and high school students throughout North America.

Litefoot is a feature film actor and has starred in such major motion pictures as, The Indian In The Cupboard and Mortal

Kombat: Annihilation. He has also appeared on the television programs: C.S.I. Miami, Family Law and Any Day Now.

Litefoot's entrepreneurial spirit has grown to include successful pursuits in the world of fashion through his popular "Native Style" clothing line. The Native Style brand enjoys distribution via Native American casinos, various retail outlets, Native American powwows and events nationwide and through its fully functional e-commerce website at: www.nativestyle.net.

In early 2010, Litefoot became the first Native American actor or musician to develop and produce his own branded line of sneakers aptly named the "Litefoot FlexArrow." His aboriginal line of footwear is the result of a joint venture collaboration with Sole Nation Health, an American Indian owned footwear company. The first pairs of the "Litefoot FlexArrow" sneaker will debut in December 2010.

Litefoot has served as co-chair of the National Indian Gaming Association's American Indian Business Network. He's served as Vice-President of Native Affairs for the Triple Five Group, owners of the world's largest retail shopping malls -- the Mall of America and the West Edmonton Mall. Litefoot has facilitated a range of business opportunities in Indian Country from casino gaming, hospitality, land development and various green energy initiatives.

Litefoot continues to constantly tour Indian Country as a popular rap artist and public speaker. Over the last four years he has traveled over 145,000 miles throughout the United States bringing hope and empowerment to over 350 Native American communities on the "Reach The Rez Tour."

By successfully walking in both the traditional and contemporary worlds, Litefoot is an example of what today's young Native Americans are encouraged to become.

Discography

1992 – The Money E.P.
1993 – Native Tongue
1994 – Seein' Red
1996 – Good Day To Die
1998 – The Clown Kutz
1998 – The Life & Times
1998 – Red Ryders Vol.1
1999 – Red Ryders Vol. 2
1999 – Rez Affiliated
1999 – The Lite Years 1989–1999 – The Best of Mr. Foot
2001 – Tribal Boogie
2002 – The Messenger
2003 – Native American Me
2004 – Redvolution
2008 – Relentless Pursuit
2011 – The Testament

Filmography

FILM	ROLE	STUDIO/DIRECTOR
The Indian in the Cupboard	Little Bear/ Lead Actor	Paramount Pictures/ Frank Oz
Mortal Kombat Annihilation	Nightwolf/ Lead Actor	New Line Cinema/ Jon Leonetti
Kull the Conqueror	Ascalante/ Lead Actor	Universal Pictures/ John Nicollela
Adaptation	Russell/ Supporting Actor	Columbia Pictures/ Spike Jonez
29 Palms	Warrior #1/ Lead Actor	Artisan/ Leonardo Ricagni
The Song of Hiawatha	Hiawatha/ Lead Actor	Hallmark Entertainment/ Jeff Shore
The Pearl	Juan Tomas/ Lead Actor	Independent/ Alfredo Zacharias

The Picture of Priority	Angel Whitecloud/ Lead Actor	Independent/ Mick Mapelli

TV SERIES/EPISODE	ROLE	NETWORK/DIRECTOR
Any Day Now/No More, Forever	Charley Majors/ Lead Actor	Lifetime Network/ Briana London
Family Law/Americans	John Grant/ Lead Actor	CBS/Elodie Keen
Any Day Now/The Real Thing	Charley Majors/ Lead Actor	Lifetime Network/Tom McLoughlin
CSI: Miami/Slow Burn	Card Dealer/Supporting Actor	CBS/Joe Chappelle

Awards

First Americans in the Arts – Outstanding Performance
Indian in the Cupboard 1995
American Indian Film Institute – Best Actor
Indian in the Cupboard 1996
First Americans in the Arts – Outstanding Performance
Kull the Conqueror 1997
Native American Music Awards- Best Rap Album
Good Day To Die 1998
Native American Music Awards- Best Rap/Hip Hop Album
The Life & Times 1999
Native American Music Awards- Best Rap/Hip Hop Album
Rez Affiliated 2000
Native American Music Awards- Best Rap/Hip Hop Album
Tribal Boogie 2002
Native American Music Awards- Best Male Artist
The Messenger 2003
Native American Music Awards- Artist of The Year
Native American Me 2004
Indian Summer Music Awards – Best Rap Album
Native American Me 2004
Indian Summer Music Awards – Best Rap Album
Redvolution 2005

Continue the journey in the next volume of
Litefoot's story in:

The Medicine of Prayer: Temptation

In bookstores beginning Summer 2011

www.litefoot.com

www.facebook.com/litefoot

www.twitter.com/litefoot

www.youtube.com/litefoot